HISTO
SHIPWRECKS

of the Southern Gulf Islands
of British Columbia

Warren Oliver Bush
Jacques Marc

Underwater Archaeological
Society of BC

 FriesenPress

Suite 300 - 990 Fort St
Victoria, BC, V8V 3K2
Canada

www.friesenpress.com

Copyright © 2020 by Jacques Marc and Warren Oliver Bush
First Edition — 2020

Front cover
Steam Tug Point Grey aground on Virago Rock in Porlier Pass, courtesy of British Columbia
Maritime Museum.

Frontispiece
1. Top left: MV *Cape Able* with UASBC divers
2. Top right: UASBC dive team with MV *Juan de Fuca Warrior*
3. Lower left: UASBC dive team plotting survey results
4. Lower right: UASBC dive team aboard MV *Cape Able*

ISBN
978-1-5255-7044-5 (Hardcover)
978-1-5255-7045-2 (Paperback)
978-1-5255-7046-9 (eBook)

1. SOCIAL SCIENCE, ARCHAEOLOGY

Distributed to the trade by The Ingram Book Company

CONTENTS

Preface

Dedication

The authors dedicate this book to the memory of Fred Rogers, British Columbia's veteran wreck diver. His first wreck dive occurred in 1955, on the steam tug *Point Grey* in the Gulf Islands. Bitten by the diving bug, he went on to explore scores of wrecks around the BC coast.

While many of his dives were for salvaging, he took copious notes and wrote three books about wreck diving. His records allow us to trace many of the early activities associated with BC shipwrecks.

About This Book

This book is the tenth in a series of regional status reports produced by the Underwater Archaeological Society of British Columbia (UASBC), with support from the Province of BC's Heritage Branch.

The report uses text, maps, drawings, and photographs to describe the historic shipwreck resources found off BC's Southern Gulf Islands. The project overview section explains the parameters, methodology, and logistics of the study, as well as the field conditions we encountered. Next, an introduction briefly outlines how the Southern Gulf Islands developed as an economic region, a settlement area, and a commercial route. Chapters on each vessel describe where and when the vessel was built, who owned it, what it did, how it was lost, and what remains. We conclude each chapter by assessing the significance of the ship and recommending any further action to help preserve the wreck sites or enhance public use of them.

The UASBC

The Underwater Archaeological Society of British Columbia is a non-profit volunteer organization founded in 1975. We are dedicated to promoting the science of underwater archaeology and to conserving, preserving, and protecting the maritime heritage lying beneath our coastal and inland waters.

The UASBC assists archaeologists by undertaking worthwhile projects that professionals are not currently addressing. Inventories of shipwrecks and other submerged cultural sites are an especially important contribution to archaeology. Information about the location, history, and status of these resources is vital for their conservation and management. The provincial Archaeology Branch, in particular, needs such data in order to establish site-management policy before a user conflict or preservation crisis arises.

UASBC reports are not just for government managers, however; they are also public education for the general reader. The ultimate goal of the UASBC is to complete a province wide inventory of underwater heritage resources.

Legal Protection of Wrecks in British Columbia

Portions or the entirety of all sites described in this report are protected under British Columbia's *Heritage Conservation Act*, as amended in 1994. The legislation was designed to prevent the loss of cultural resources. Any disturbance of a shipwreck (or aircraft wreck) more than two years old requires a written permit from the provincial Archaeology Branch. The act expressly forbids artifact collection of vessel parts, cargo, and personal effects. Unauthorized modification or destruction of these sites, artifact removal, excavation, or similar activities is a criminal offence with personal fines of up to $50,000 and corporate fines of up to $2,000,000. The *Heritage Conservation Act* does not prevent sport diving, photography, or non-disturbance archaeological activity on wreck sites.

Warren Oliver Bush and Jacques Marc 2020

Acknowledgments

While no specific provincial grants were forthcoming for this project, the Underwater Archaeological Society of British Columbia would like to thank the Province of BC's Heritage Branch, in particular its director, Richard Linzey, for providing ongoing contract work that indirectly facilitated the completion of this project.

We are indebted to Erin and Julie Bradley of Emerald Ocean Charters for providing their vessels, the *Juan de Fuca Warrior* and MV *Cape Able*, at a nominal rate, ensuring that we could complete this project. Thanks also to Lyle Berzins of Stellar Marine for assisting with his vessel *Miss Emily*.

Thanks to David W. Griffiths for his original research and documentation of the Gulf Island wrecks in the 1982 report. It provided many valuable insights as to what work the UASBC completed in the Gulf Islands in the late 1970s and early 1980s.

Jacques Marc, Ewan Anderson, and Dean Driver provided underwater still photography – thank you.

We can't thank Ewan Anderson enough for his contribution to this project. He introduced the concept of photogrammetry to the documentation work and produced an excellent site plan and model for the *Del Norte*.

The Parks Canada Underwater Archaeological Services unit, in particular Jonathan Moore, Ryan Harris, and Thierry Boyer, assisted us by completing searches for the *Admiral Knight* and documenting the *Henry Foss* with their high-resolution multi-beam equipment.

Thank you to Craig Lessels and Patrick McNeill, hydrographers with the Canadian Hydrographic Service (CHS), for looking through CHS multi-beam data in Trincomali channel for potential *Emily Harris* targets. Thanks also to Duncan Havens of CHS for sharing imagery and the location information for multiple small wrecks within the Gulf Island Study Area.

Many people deserve recognition for assisting us with research. "Mr. Shipwreck" himself, Fred Rogers, freely provided information about his trips to the Gulf Islands in the 1960s before his passing.

From elsewhere: James Shuttleworth and Robert Schwemmer in California and Michael Skalley in Washington responded to research requests.

A particularly hearty "thanks" is in order to Lea Edgar of the Vancouver Maritime Museum and Alicia Barnes of the Puget Sound Maritime Historical Society. They showed patience and fortitude in dealing with a never-ending stream of research queries.

We are grateful to the institutions that provided information and photographs to this project:

- Australian National Maritime Museum
- Royal BC Museum, BC Archives
- City of Vancouver Archives
- Del Norte County Historical Society – Karen Betlejewski
- J. Porter Shaw Library at San Francisco Maritime National Historic Park – Gina Bardi
- Maine Maritime Museum – Anne Farrow
- Mystic Seaport's The Museum of America and the Sea, along with its online registers
- National Archives and Records Administration Pacific Northwest Region (Seattle) – Brita Merkel
- Puget Sound Maritime Historical Society – Alicia Barnes
- Vancouver Maritime Museum – Lea Edgar

- Maritime Museum of British Columbia – Judy Thompson
- Medford Historical Society & Museum
- North Vancouver Museum and Archives – Jessica Bushey

Many other online resources were also readily available from institutions around the world by simply typing a ship name, shipyard, or owner into a search engine and letting the internet do its magic.

This publication could not have happened without the dedicated cadre of UASBC divers who participated in survey expeditions from 2015 to 2019. The following list includes 17 divers who participated in two or more expeditions, in alphabetical order: Ewan Anderson, Tyler Armeneau, Keith Bossons, Greg Bossons, Warren Oliver Bush, Dean Driver, Damien Harabalja, Holger Heitland, Jiri Kotler, Jacques Marc, John Middleton, Bob Simpson, Aurora Skala, George Silvestrini, Paul Spencer, Bronwen Young, and Eric Young. Many others joined us for a single trip.

Finally, we would like to thank David Hill Turner for contributing heavily to the writing of the History of Shipping in the Gulf Islands.

Project Overview

Introduction

The UASBC completed its first historic shipwreck inventory project on the BC coast in 1982, focusing on the Southern Gulf Islands. To meet a funding requirement, we collated the research and diving results from that project into a technical report for the BC Heritage Trust.

Today the Southern Gulf Islands are a popular diving destination, and divers and historians often ask the UASBC for information on local wrecks. While our more recent inventories are publicly available, we never published the 1982 Gulf Islands report as it was not written for that purpose. Also, new discoveries and changes to existing sites warranted additional research and diving. Consequently, the UASBC decided to re-inventory the historic wrecks in the Southern Gulf Islands area and publish the results.

Objectives

The Southern Gulf Island re-inventory project had two objectives:

1. To locate, identify, and assess what submerged cultural resources remain in the area.
2. To archaeologically document selected shipwrecks for the Province of BC's Heritage and Archaeology Branches, and making our report publicly available to historians, divers, and the general public.

Geographic Parameters

The name "Gulf Islands" comes from the Gulf of Georgia, the original name used by Captain George Vancouver in his mapping of the southern part of the archipelago.

For the purpose of this project, the Southern Gulf Islands are defined as the area extending 76 km from the north end of Gabriola Island to East Point on Saturna Island in the south, and encompassing the archipelago of islands between Vancouver Island and the Strait of Georgia.

Site Selection

The first step in any shipwreck survey is to determine what vessels were lost in the region, and which of those to study.

The UASBC derived the initial list of wrecks for study from our 1982 Gulf Islands report. Jacques Marc selected additional wrecks after consulting Transport Canada's *List of Shipping Casualties Resulting in Total Loss in British Columbia Coastal Waters Since 1897*, the Hubert Lindsay Cadieux Wreck Series List at the City of Vancouver Archives, Bill Cramer's unpublished 1990 *Compendium of Vessels Wrecked in B.C.*, and Shipwreck Chart No. 3 in Fred Rogers' *Shipwrecks of British Columbia*. We learned that more than 40 vessels were lost within or near the Gulf Islands.

To reduce this list to a practical number of vessels to study, we decided to focus on major vessels that were more than 75 feet long and lost before 1960. While smaller vessels like fishing vessels and tugs are an equally significant part of British Columbia's maritime history, they are too numerous and difficult to find. Small vessels are equally protected by the *Heritage Conservation Act*.

The UASBC initially considered eighteen vessels for the study, and ultimately reduced the final number to a more manageable fourteen. The four omitted vessels were:

- The schooner *Victoria Packet*, a small vessel taken by First Nations near Porlier Pass in 1860. The actual location is unknown.
- The 85-foot steamship *Champion*, which burned on Holland Flats near Ladysmith in 1903. All that is left is its keel.
- The 65-foot wooden tug *Peggy McNeill*, which was

tragically lost in Porlier Pass in 1923. Due to deep waters and a strong current, it's unlikely it can be found.

- The 82-foot steamship *Oscar*, which blew up in its entirety off Protection Island in 1913 and little is thought to survive. The UASBC searched for it using side-scan sonar without success in 2007.

Site Location Map

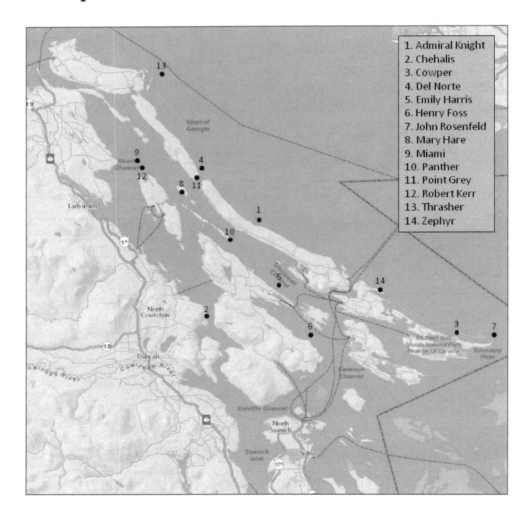

1. Admiral Knight
2. Chehalis
3. Cowper
4. Del Norte
5. Emily Harris
6. Henry Foss
7. John Rosenfeld
8. Mary Hare
9. Miami
10. Panther
11. Point Grey
12. Robert Kerr
13. Thrasher
14. Zephyr

Historical Research

The next step was to determine the history of each vessel and find information on its wrecking location. The 1982 report provided relative descriptions of where some of the wrecks could be found, but did not provide precise coordinates. Global positioning was not available at the time. To locate many of the wrecks and to find new sites, we relied on archival research and consulting marine historians and

divers. In many cases, divers who had previously located or visited a wreck site were able to pinpoint the location on a map. This significantly reduced the time we had to spend searching.

For sites not yet located (*Admiral Knight, Cowper, Emily Harris* and *Mary Hare*), the UASBC relied on archival research to define the search area. We reviewed historic newspaper accounts about the wrecking events for potential location information. Warren Oliver Bush researched eight vessels, and Jacques Marc researched the remaining six vessels.

Fieldwork Logistics

UASBC Explorations Director Jacques Marc and members of the Explorations Committee organized all fieldwork and related logistics. As principal investigator, Jacques was responsible for assigning tasks to dive teams, analyzing the data they collected, drawing site plans, and compiling the final report.

Most of the Gulf Islands are readily accessible by high-speed day boats. As a result, most of the fieldwork was completed through day trips and completing two dives per diver on each trip. This worked well for completing searches, but day trips didn't provide the time needed for adequate surveying. Consequently, we organized two multi-day expeditions to focus on surveying.

The first surveying expedition took place 23-26 September 2016 to complete datum offset surveys on the *Panther* and *Del Norte* wrecks. The second expedition between 7-9 April 2017 focused on surveying the *Robert Kerr*. The longer trips allowed us to establish baselines and to complete survey work through repeated dives.

For the day trips, we sailed aboard the *Juan de Fuca Warrior*, a fast aluminum dive boat operated by Erin and Julie Bradley. For the two expeditions, we used the 50-foot MV *Cape Able*, also operated by Erin and Julie Bradley. Conover Cove, Wallace Island became our base of operations for the expeditions because it was central to the wrecks being surveyed (the *Robert Kerr*, *Panther*, and *Del Norte*). Holger Heitland, Eric and Bronwen Young, and Keith Bossons supplied their personal vessels for accommodation. We then used the *Cape Able* to transport divers to the various wreck sites.

From October 2015 to September 2019, the UASBC spent twenty days diving within the Gulf Islands, searching for and documenting the wrecks, and completing 238 person-dives. This number does not include several preparation dives done before 2015. During these dives, the divers undertook all survey work, topside support, and photography, and also provided their own diving gear.

The divers' working depths ranged from 5 m (for the tug *Chehalis*) to 35 m (for the *Henry Foss*). At many locations, including *Henry Foss*, *Del Norte*, *Point Grey*, *Cowper*, *John Rosenfeld* and *Thrasher*, we had to plan dives for slack current. Water temperature below the surface thermocline was consistently 4°C, requiring a dry suit for working dives.

Underwater visibility varied depending on the season. During fall and winter dives, the visibility was generally 6-8 m. After the spring plankton bloom, the visibility would drop to 3-4 m or less. The underwater visibility on the *Henry Foss* was never more than 1-2 m.

Search Methods

In many cases the UASBC had advance knowledge about where to look for the wrecks based on past work. In several cases, including *Admiral Knight*, *Cowper*, *Chehalis*, *Mary Hare* and *Emily Harris*, we conducted searches to try find the wrecks. We used multi-beam and side-scan technologies to search for the *Emily Harris* and *Admiral Knight*; in the remaining cases, we conducted diver swim searches.

Generally, we put search teams in the water at intervals. Divers were given instructions to follow a compass bearing or a depth contour. If they found the wreck, they were to release a numbered float. We recorded entry and exit positions and float locations by global positioning system (GPS).

Once we found a wreck, we did a visual reconnaissance of the site. This established the boundaries of the site and located prominent wreck features such as the anchor, capstan, engine, rudder, and propeller. We marked the artifacts' locations with buoys and pinpointed their positions with by GPS.

Additional dives sought to obtain as much data from each site as possible with the equipment, time, and personnel available. We used non-destructive methods only, including mapping, 35-mm digital photography, and video.

Archaeological Documentation

In this project, we found and explored ten of fourteen sites. We searched for the *Admiral Knight, Cowper, Mary Hare* and *Emily Harris*, but did not find them.

We made new site maps for three of the wrecks: the *Panther, Robert Kerr,* and *Del Norte.* We reused the original *Zephyr* site plan because twice we were unable to dive the site due to weather conditions.

To map a site, we laid down a fibreglass tape measure along the centre of the wreck or through the middle of the debris field. We determined artifact positions by taking offset measurements from that baseline. In some cases, divers used tri-lateration to improve accuracy.

Once the artifact locations had been plotted, divers measured and sketched the pieces. These techniques enabled us to produce a scale drawing from only a few dives. The level of detail in the site maps varies depending on the amount of time allotted to them, and the plans record only what was visible on the sea floor. In some cases, we know that much more is buried in the sea bottom.

Work on the *Henry Foss* was initially limited to photography and GPS because of its depth and the poor underwater visibility. On 9 May 2019, the Parks Canada Underwater Archaeology Unit assisted the UASBC by completing a multi-beam survey on the *Henry Foss.*

Dive teams used photogrammetry on the *Del Norte, Point Grey,* and *Robert Kerr* to record the position and condition of artifacts. This is described in greater detail in the *Del Norte* chapter.

Both metric and imperial measures are used in this report. Maps and field notes are in metric, as is archaeological practice. Figures from historic documents, such as ship dimensions, are transcribed verbatim in imperial units. Water depths are given in feet because diver depth gauges in North America read that way. To know what the depth relates to, we specify the tide height at the time the depth of water was measured.

Latitude and longitude co-ordinates are generally presented in the format that marine GPS sets give them: in degrees, minutes, and decimal seconds (hundredths of a second). Readers who prefer traditional seconds can convert decimal seconds to seconds by multiplying the numbers after the decimal point by 0.06. GPS co-ordinates are not necessarily given for all of the wrecks.

Compass directions are true bearings, adjusted for magnetic declination.

This project observed a strict no-disturbance policy. Project divers did not remove artifacts from the wrecks and they did not excavate.

The Wrecks

In the chapters that follow, fourteen wrecks are described in alphabetical order. Some accounts are brief since the location of the wreck remains unknown or the vessel was not well documented in archival sources. Other chapters are lengthy, particularly if the vessel was well-known or the underwater site required a long description.

Foreign vessels make up the largest component of the wrecks in the Gulf Island study area. Nine vessels were registered in the United States and five were registered in Canada.

Sailing ships make up the single largest category. All the sailing ships were made of wood. Four were full rigged ships (square-rigged on all masts), one was a barque, and one was a cut-down barque. The *Cowper, Panther,* and *Zephyr* were under sail when wrecked. The *Thrasher, Rosenfeld,* and *Robert Kerr* were under tow when they grounded. Five of the sailing ships carried coal cargoes, while the *Zephyr* carried sandstone from Newcastle Island.

Steamers represent the next largest category of vessels in the study area. Of the five steamers, four were made of wood (the *Admiral Knight, Emily Harris, Mary Hare,* and *Del Norte*). Only the *Miami* was made of steel. The *Miami* was loaded with coal when it strayed off course and grounded. The *Admiral Knight* was transiting through BC waters when it caught fire and burned. The *Del Norte* went aground while backing out of Porlier Pass, the *Emily Harris* suffered an explosion and sank, and the *Mary Hare* burned. The *Emily Harris* and *Mary Hare* were local vessels transporting people and cargoes. The *Del Norte* was transiting from Nanaimo to San Francisco with coal and passengers.

Three tugs are represented in the study area. Two were steam powered and one was diesel. The *Chehalis* and *Henry Foss* were wooden while the *Point Grey* was made of steel. The *Chehalis* and *Point Grey* were towing payloads (logs and barges), while the *Henry Foss* was transiting from Port Angeles to Ladysmith to pick up a tow.

Two lives were lost in the *Zephyr* sinking, three lives were lost in the *Emily Harris* explosion, and six lives were lost when the *Henry Foss* foundered.

Ten vessels were lost before 1900, and six vessels were lost during or after 1900. The earliest wreck is the *Del Norte* of 1868, while the most recent wreck was the *Henry Foss*, lost in 1959.

Half of the ships lost in the study area were carrying coal cargoes and were bound for San Francisco. This is significant, as the late 1800s represent the zenith of coal production in Ladysmith and Nanaimo.

The most enigmatic wreck in this project is the yet-to-be-found steamer *Emily Harris*, whose loss in 1871 remains shrouded in mystery.

A Brief History of Shipping in the Southern Gulf Islands

The Southern Gulf Islands form a network of channels and islands between Vancouver Island and the mainland. While the islands offer shelter to marine traffic, their reefs, rocks, strong currents and sometimes-limited visibility have contributed to the demise of vessels large and small.

It may seem unusual that most of the larger vessels wrecked throughout the Gulf Islands were carrying coal. While lumber and fish immediately come to mind to most residents, coal was the first bulk cargo to be transported from what became British Columbia.

For thousands of years before the arrival of European explorers, the islands were home to the Coast Salish peoples. Evidence of their presence is traced through middens, petroglyphs, human remains and artifacts. The Snuneymuxw occupied the shores of Departure Bay, Nanaimo Harbour and Gabriola Island. The Lyackson Mustimuhw resided on Valdes Island and the Stz'uminus occupied territory on east Vancouver Island, bordering the Strait of Georgia and Ladysmith Harbour. Penelakut villages were found on Penelakut Island, Galiano Island, and near the mouth of the Chemainus River on Vancouver Island. The Cowichan were further south and occupied the Cowichan Valley.

When the first Europeans arrived in the summer of 1791, they encountered the Snuneymuxw on Gabriola Island. Jose Maria Narvaez and Francisco de Eliza did some minor trading when they stopped to fill their water barrels. The following summer, Spain launched a more active survey of the inside waters under the command of Dionisio Alcala Galiano and Cayetano Valdes Flores. They departed San Blas, Mexico, in March 1792 and sailed to Nootka Sound aboard the *Sutil* and *Mexicana*. In June 1792, they anchored at the port of Nunez Gaona (Neah Bay) and, guided by First Nation chief Tetacu, they crossed to Vancouver Island where they began charting the waters around the Gulf Islands.

On 21 June 1792, the Spaniards sighted and met up with Captain George Vancouver's *Discovery* and *Chatham* near present-day Point Grey. Many of the islands, channels, bays, harbours and other natural features now carry the names of English and Spanish explorers who carried out the surveys: Narvaez Bay, Vesuvius Bay, and Dionisio Point, for example, were named during their joint surveys. In 1794, Captain Vancouver negotiated the final Nootka Convention that transferred Vancouver Island and, by extension, the Gulf Islands, from Spain to Great Britain.

In 1827, the Hudson's Bay Company (HBC) ship *Cadboro*, using charts created by Vancouver, sailed through the Gulf Islands and up the Fraser River to establish Fort Langley. Nine years after that, the company's coastal fleet welcomed the *Beaver*, the first steamship on the North Pacific. The crews of HBC boats added considerably to our knowledge of coastal waters, as they navigated regularly from Fort Nisqually in southern Puget Sound to the Russian headquarters at Sitka, Alaska. In 1843, following the creation of the international boundary west of the Rocky Mountains along the forty-ninth parallel, the HBC moved its Columbia Department headquarters from Fort Vancouver on the Columbia River to Fort Victoria.

The discovery of gold near San Francisco in 1848 brought waves of gold-seekers across the continent and by sea around Cape Horn. Steam engines were beginning to replace sailing ships on long voyages and the engines needed coal to produce power. The only known deposits were at the north end of Vancouver Island at Fort Rupert, near present-day Port Hardy. The HBC introduced skilled miners from Scotland to mine the coal. It was of poor quality, however, and pleased neither ship owners nor miners.

In the spring of 1850, Snuneymuxw Chief Che-wich-i-kan (or Ki-et-sa-kun) noticed the blacksmith at Fort Victoria burning coal in his forge. After learning that it came by ship from faraway England, he commented that "the rock that burned" was also found on the beach near where he lived. He was promised a reward if he brought a good sample of coal, which he did several months later. HBC Governor James Douglas dispatched clerk Joseph William McKay, an amateur geologist, to the area to confirm the coal and to claim it for the HBC. Shortly afterward, the company transferred their miners from Fort Rupert to Nanaimo (then Colviletown) to begin mining coal.

In September 1852, the HBC ship *Cadboro* was loaded with 480 barrels of coal. The coal was transported to the anchored ship by the Snuneymuxw in cedar baskets at a rate of one two-and-a-half-point blanket and other goods for every twenty barrels of coal. Shortly afterward, an American ship was also loaded with coal in the harbour. The industrial revolution had finally reached the shores of British Columbia.

Keen to exploit the new resource, the HBC moved more men and their families into the Nanaimo area. Ships sailed north from San Francisco, often a two-week voyage, and carefully made their way through the straits to Nanaimo, all under sail. Navigation information came from the same charts created years earlier by Captain Vancouver.

HBC men sometimes served as pilots, providing local information to masters unfamiliar with the waters. More boats entered active service in 1858 as prospectors discovered gold on the lower Fraser River and, in the early 1860s, sawmills began to export lumber from Burrard Inlet.

Navigating the Gulf Islands was hazardous. Fog, wind, strong currents, and no aids to navigation led to many wrecks. Recognizing that mariners needed better charts, the Royal Navy dispatched Captain G. H. Richards in 1857 to conduct a more detailed hydrographic survey of the region. For the next six summers, Richards and his crew added considerably to our knowledge of local waters. His lengthy reports to London also detailed his recommendations for lighthouses, buoys and harbours.

It was the heavily laden colliers – ships carrying coal – that seemed to have the worst luck navigating the channels around the islands. Many features such as Panther Point, Thrasher Rock, and Rosenfeld Rock mark the locations where the voyage of a loaded collier ended abruptly.

The lure of free land and opportunity began to attract increasing numbers of people to the area. A network of small boats such as the *Mary Hare*, the *Iroquois*, and the *Emily Harris* moved people, cargo and livestock between settlements, often regardless of the weather. Unenforced regulations also led to tragic accidents, such as when the overloaded *Iroquois* capsized near Sidney in 1911.

As you read this report, more stories will unfold that serve to remind us that not so long ago, travelling by ship along the BC coast was a prospect fraught with danger.

Edited by David Hill Turner

SS *Admiral Knight*

SS *Portland*, courtesy Puget Sound Maritime Historical Society (Williamson Collection, Neg. no. 2877.)

Official Number: 214059

Signal Letters: LGBF

Registry: United States

Construction

In 1915, Seattle shipbuilders Johnson Brothers and Blanchard were awarded a contract to build a 150-foot twin-screw wooden ship that could carry thirty-five passengers and 700 tons of freight. Not having previously built anything as large and heavy, the firm under-bid the contract and went bankrupt during its construction. Blanchard was paid by the receiver to finish the job.

On the evening of 23 April 1916, the Westward Navigation Company of Seattle launched the $70,000 motor ship *Kuskokwim River*. Ten-year-old Helen J. Graham christened the vessel as her father, John Graham, a well-known architect and owner of the vessel, proudly watched. Instead of sliding gracefully, the ship stuck fast on the ways and had to be pulled into the water. Built of wood, the vessel had a single deck, two masts, and a sharp head and round stern. Its registered dimensions were 142.2 feet long, 35.7 feet wide and 12.3 feet deep. It measured 643 gross tons and 506 net tons. At the time of its launch, it was fitted with two Meitz & Weiss three-cylinder semi-diesel engines, two shafts and two screws. Each engine generated 150hp for a combined horsepower of 300. The cargo and anchor winches were electrically driven.

The *Kuskokwim River* was designed by naval architect L. E. (Ted) Leary for the Westward Navigation Co. to provide freight service between Puget Sound and the Kuskokwim River. On 10 May 1916, Captain Walter Tinn applied for an official number, which the Collector of Customs responded to by bestowing 'Official Number 214059.' Additionally, the Port of Seattle issued a Certificate of Registry No. 339 in the name of the Westward Navigation Company on 24 May 1916.

Early in 1917, the vessel was re-engined with two quadruple expansion steam engines. Following this modification, the vessel was registered as a steamship. A 1920 *Johnson's Steam Vessel* publication records that the engine cylinder diameters were 11, 19, 23, and 23 inches, and it had a 15-inch stroke. The engines generated 518 imperial hp. Two water tube boilers that measured 9 feet by 8.8 feet and had a 175-lb working pressure powered the steam engines.

The November 1916 issue of *The Wireless Age* records that the *Kuskokwim River* was recently equipped with a Marconi Apparatus and issued call letters WLK.

Operational History

Very little of the early operational history of the SS *Admiral Knight* could be found.

Fred Rogers recounts that on its maiden voyage to Alaska, the vessel was stranded in the Kuskokwim River and was towed to Seattle for repairs. Following repairs, it made another start for Alaska, but about 60 miles from Cape Flattery it caught fire and was saved and taken to Port Angeles. Although most of its cargo was ruined, the ship was repaired, then held for salvage costs.

A Washington State court case *McCreery vs. Graham* identified that there were early issues with the

semi-diesel engines. According to the court case, John Graham (Westward Navigation Company) entered into a contract with H. W. McCreery to furnish and install two marine engines in Graham's vessel. The engines were installed but Graham claimed that the use of the vessel was not satisfactory because of the engines' condition and quality. Graham needed the engines repaired so that he could sell the vessel. After receiving assurances from the court that the engines would be put in good working order by McCreery, Graham sold the vessel and its engines on 22 January 1917.

On 22 February 1917, Salem, Oregon's *The Daily Capital Journal* recorded the incorporation of the Alaska Oregon Steamship Company for the purpose of building, owning and operating steam, gas and sailing vessels. The incorporating officers were Charles A. Burckhardt, F. O. Burckhardt and Lawrence A. McNary. The place of business was Portland.

On 4 April 1917, the Certificate of Registry No. 339 issued at Seattle was surrendered and a new registration document, Temporary Registry No. 410, was issued to the newly incorporated Alaska Oregon Steamship Company of Portland Oregon. The reasons given for the change of registry were that the vessel name was changed from *Kuskokwin River* to SS *Portland*, the rig changed from diesel to steam, the net tonnage dropped from 506 to 348 tons, and the district changed from Seattle to Portland.

On 28 February 1919, the SS *Portland* was sold to Alaska Pacific Fisheries of Portland, Oregon, where C. A. Burckhardt was president. Alaska Pacific Fisheries operated a number of canneries between 1911 and 1925, including Yes Bay, Burnett Inlet, and Chomly in Southeast Alaska. The company needed a vessel to service these canneries. That being said, a month later on 25 March, the SS *Portland* was renamed SS *Admiral Knight* in honour of Austin M. Knight, a rear admiral in the American Navy, and three days later Permanent Registration No. 367 was issued to the Pacific Steamship Company (Admiral Line). The reason given was that the vessel had changed hands and district.

On 29 March 1919, *The Seattle Star* announced that the *Admiral Knight* would sail with a full cargo of cannery supplies to southeastern Alaska. This would be the *Admiral Knight*'s first trip under the Pacific Steamship Company flag. The steamer appears to have made regular runs to Alaska for the next couple of months.

In early May, the vessel was recorded in Milbank Sound headed south, and on 5 May it was at the Grand Trunk Pacific dock in Seattle. On 6 May, it travelled to Anacortes, presumably to load cargo, and was recorded heading north past Bella Bella on 10 May. It was still northbound passing Petersburg on 12 May. On 18 May, the *Knight* was sighted in Queen Charlotte Sound, headed south. By 21 May, the vessel was moored at Seattle's Pier 4.

The *Admiral Knight* was next observed northbound off Egg Island on 24 May and was then seen southbound off Cape Lazo on 31 May. On 2 June 1919, the *Admiral Knight* was recorded as arriving at Seattle from southeastern Alaska. Following its return on 2 June, the *Admiral Knight* appears to have been laid up for the next two months. *The Seattle Star* Marine Movements section records the vessel consistently at Pier A in Seattle for all of June and July 1919, up until its final voyage.

Loss

The *Admiral Knight* departed Seattle at midnight on Saturday, 26 July 1919, bound for Ketchikan with a cargo of lumber and empty barrels. Other reports state it was carrying a load of creosoted piles and 400 barrels of fuel oil.

On Sunday evening shortly after 17:00 while off Sand Heads, assistant engineer A. O. Nyberg discovered fire shooting out of the engine room. He immediately gave the alarm and called first mate John Weabust, who in turn contacted the chief engineer. Chief Engineer Goranson recounted that he climbed down the ladder leading to the engine room but was blocked by a mass of smoke and fire that nearly enveloped him. He said that he met Nyberg carrying the prostrate form of B. Neitson, a fireman who was seriously burned, and Goranson helped both men reach the main deck.

Once everyone was on deck, Captain Allen ordered seventeen crewmen and Goranson into the lifeboat.

Goranson recounted that the ship was running in circles at about 6 or 7 knots, as there had not been time to shut off the engines. He said that the lifeboat nearly capsized upon being launched. The captain and five men remained aboard the burning ship because there wasn't enough room in the lifeboat. The only other boat aboard, a small skiff, had swamped during efforts to launch it.

The Canadian Pacific Railway (CPR) ship the *Princess Victoria*, on its regular run from Victoria to Vancouver, was off the Fraser River when First Officer N. J. Sterner heard several faint whistles coming from a ship that was acting strangely five miles on the *Victoria*'s port beam. The CPR vessel bore down on it and found the *Knight* in flames and six men standing on the forecastle. Coming as close as they dared to the flaming hulk, the *Victoria*'s crew sent a boat across the water and took off the last six men, averting a catastrophe. As they jumped in the lifeboat of the *Princess Victoria*, the stack of the burning ship collapsed and the men reported hearing an explosion. The *Victoria* also picked up the lifeboat loaded with the other members of the crew.

The injured fireman was given medical assistance on the *Victoria* and was rushed to St. Paul's Hospital when the steamer reached Vancouver. He was reported to be in critical condition but did survive. The *Victoria* transported the remaining crew members to Seattle, arriving there at 07:00 on Monday, 28 July 1919.

The fire is believed to have resulted from a backfire from the burner when the fires were being changed.

When the *Victoria* left Vancouver late on Sunday night for Seattle, the derelict *Admiral Knight* was still afloat and burning. A notice to mariners was put out to this effect on 29 July, reading

> The Department of Marine has received the following information from Capt. Griffin Master of the *Princess Victoria*, dated July 28: The hulk of the steamer *Admiral Knight* bearing six (6) miles south by west from the Sand Heads lightship, Gulf of Georgia. Vessel still burning.

The Vancouver Dredging and Salvage Company lost

no time in putting men alongside the burning ship by 27 July, and by Monday, 28 July, they reported that it was very low in the stern when they let it go, thinking it would sink. A search party led by Mr. A. B. Graham of the Pacific Steamship Company went out on the tugboat *Dominion* on Tuesday, 29 July. The search party cruised from the spot where the crew were rescued – 6 miles southwest of Sand Heads Lighthouse – to the entrance of Active Pass, and found no trace of the vessel. The 30 July *Daily Colonist* reported that no sign of the derelict had been seen on Monday, and they speculated the vessel had exploded.

Captain McGregor of the Victoria Tug Company stated that his experience in those waters made him certain that the derelict had remained afloat. It would have drifted down among the islands on the American side towards Boundary Bay, following a current that runs continuously in that direction down the coastline. Captain McGregor contended that the *Admiral Knight* would not drift toward Active Pass. The 6 August *Daily Colonist* stated that there was little likelihood of the wreck of the *Admiral Knight*, which burned to the water's edge the previous week off the mouth of the Fraser River, being located for some time. The vessel was last seen one mile off Cowichan Gap (Porlier Pass) and was assumed to have sunk in deep water.

Salvage

No salvage is known to have occurred as the vessel vanished the day after the fire. Those who dived it in 1958 did not report recovering any artifacts.

Search and Discovery

The *Admiral Knight* was forgotten until the late 1950s, when a cod fisherman Andy (Henry) Crocker snagged his gear on parts of a wreck. Crocker showed island divers Lloyd Wade, Jim Polchard, Sonny Hodgeson, and Alex McCracken the potential wreck location. In 1958, they dived to 180 feet where they found a wreck. It was reported to be resting on even keel in Cable Bay on the east side of Galiano Island, opposite Retreat Cove.

Lloyd Wade, in an interview on 23 April 2006, described the wreck as a large intact hull with some house works.

He said that the hull was intact with a large forward hatch and that the dive team saw some machinery. The deck was reportedly at 180 feet and the bottom at 210 feet. There was not much more he could add, as he said that nitrogen narcosis severely impaired the dive team.

The UASBC launched a search for the *Admiral Knight* on 8 April 2006. It was our assumption based on the last sighting of the vessel (Cowichan Gap) and the information provided by Lloyd Wade that that the *Admiral Knight* rested somewhere off Cable Bay on Galiano Island. The UASBC chartered the MV *Gwaii Haanas* under the command of John Robin to conduct a search for the wreck. We travelled from Maple Bay to Cable Bay on the east side of Galiano Island to the reported location of the wreck. SAVI Marine, operated by Mike Clement of Sechelt, supplied the side-scan sonar for our search.

We reached Cable Bay at about 11:00 and deployed the side-scan sonar. We travelled pre-defined transects 2 km in length by 100 m apart, continuously watching the computer monitor for any images of what could be the *Admiral Knight*. After four hours of searching we failed to find anything in Cable Bay. We briefly checked the two smaller bays to the south but found nothing.

In spring 2019, Parks Canada's Underwater Archaeology Services Team was doing an orientation cruise with their research vessel MV *David Thompson* in the Gulf Islands. Jacques Marc, UASBC explorations director, was invited on board as a UASBC representative to learn about the ship's capabilities and to help familiarize Parks Canada staff with the shipwrecks within the proposed Southern Gulf Islands marine protected area. Jacques identified a number of uncompleted UASBC projects. One of the projects on the list was to continue the search for the *Admiral Knight*. Jonathan Moore, the project director, agreed to spend some time on a multi-beam survey search for the wreck. Thierry Boyer operated the bulti-beam on this trip.

On 14 May 2019, the *David Thompson* travelled to Cable Bay on the east side of Galiano Island. A multi-beam survey uses an array of sounders to digitize the seafloor in 3D, producing an underwater topography map. Shipwrecks will usually stand out as they appear different than the surrounding topography. Before surveying, the multi-beam was calibrated by sampling the local water to determine the speed of sound in the survey area.

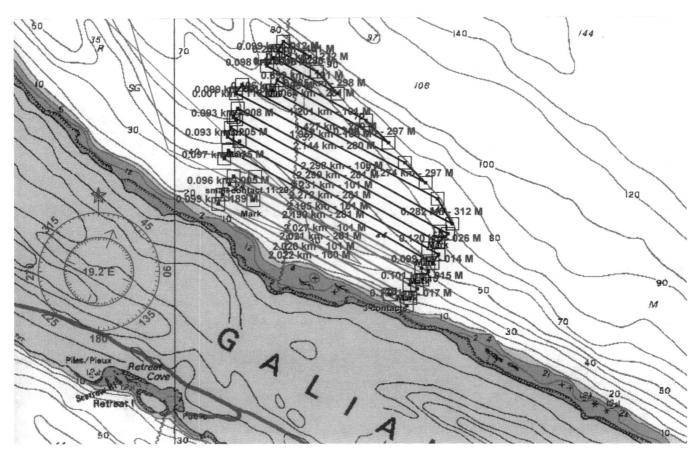

Lines highlighted in grey were searched by side scan on 8 April 2006; the black lines were not.

The *David Thompson* completed dozens of transects 3 km long starting in 60 m of water and finishing in 20 m of water. The survey began at 10:00 and concluded at 16:00. We learned that in the deeper water (30 m and greater), the bottom was primarily sand/shell and nothing of significance materialized. The bottom in the inshore waters (30 m and shallower) consisted of shelving rock. Despite a high-resolution search at 450 kHz, we did not locate anything that could have been the *Admiral Knight*.

As luck would have it, we were just in the middle of writing up this report when Craig Lessels of the Canadian Hydrographic Service contacted Jacques on 30 August 2019. He reported that he had found a target that could potentially be the *Admiral Knight*. The target, 44 m (144 feet) long sits in 57 m (187 feet) of water 1.26 km off the shore of Cable Bay.

It looks like the UASBC may have just missed the wreck during its 2006 side-scan sonar search.

Status

Despite now having a potential position for the wreck, the UASBC has not confirmed that it is a wreck, nor that it is in fact the *Admiral Knight*. The multi-beam image is not particularly compelling as it is low resolution and the wreck lies in deeper water. It is possible that the target is geography or another wreck.

Conclusions and Recommendations

The UASBC is encouraged to investigate the target off Cable Bay as soon as possible to confirm whether it is in fact the *Admiral Knight* or another vessel.

References

Admiral Knight Cargo Ship 1916-1919 Wreck https://wrecksite.eu/wreck.aspx?253921

Daily Colonist, 29 July 1919.

Ibid., 30 July 1919.

Ibid., 6 August 1919.

Brown, Giles T. *Ships That Sail No More: Marine Transportation from San Diego to Puget Sound, 1910-1940* (Lexington, 1966).

Blanchard, Norman C. and Wilen, Stephen. *Knee Deep in Shavings: Memories of Early Yachting and Boat Building on the West Coast* (Victoria, 1999).

Ellensburg Daily Record, 28 July 1919.

Johnson, Eads. *Johnson's Steam Vessels of the Atlantic, Gulf and Pacific Coasts: 1920.* (London: Forgotten Books, 2017).

List of Merchant Vessels of the United States, 1916-1919.

Newell, Gordon, ed. *The H. W. McCurdy Marine History of the Pacific Northwest: 1895-1965,* (Seattle: Superior Publishing Co., 1963), 284-308.

Railway and Marine News, 1916, 31.

Rogers, Fred. *Shipwrecks of British Columbia* (Vancouver, 1976), 42-43.

Rogers, Fred. "The MV *Admiral Knight.*" *Foghorn*, Vol. 13, No. 2 (2002), 4.

The Daily Capital Journal, 22 February 1917.

The Seattle Star, 2 May 1919.

Ibid., 13 May 1919.

Ibid., 20 May 1919.

Ibid., 9 July 1919.

Ibid., 12 July 1919.

Ibid., 16 July 1919.

Ibid., 23 July 1919.

Ibid., 24 July 1919.

The Wireless Age, Vol. 4, (New York: Marconi Publishing Corporation, 1916), 115.

https://classicyacht.org/research/classic-boat-builders-blanchard-boat-company

http://courts.mrsc.org/washreports/121WashReport/121WashReport0466.htm

Steam Tug *Chehalis*

Steam Tug *Chehalis* moored on calm water, courtesy of Puget Sound Maritime History Society Neg# 482-1.

Official Number: 126682 (United States)
Official Number: 150553 (Canada)

Construction

Gray's Harbor Commercial Company built and launched the *Chehalis* on 7 November 1890 in what was then Cosmopolis, Chehalis County, Washington State. Prince Edward Island-born master carpenter Neil Cooney oversaw construction, and designed the vessel as a one-masted and one-decked wooden steam tug, 73 feet 6 inches long, 16 feet wide, and 7 feet 6 inches deep. The *Chehalis* was equipped with a compound steam engine with cylinders measuring 22 and 10 ¼ inches, with a 12-inch stroke. The engine generated 19.63 nominal horse power and provided a maximum speed of 7 knots. A Scotch Marine boiler built by the Reid Brothers of Bellingham, Washington, in 1905, generated steam. The dimensions of the boiler are unknown, but the boiler space was 20 feet long. *Chehalis* displaced 68.8 gross tons or 39 registered tons, and had a straight head and

rounded stern.

Operational History

Chehalis initially transported log booms, passengers and freight in and around Gray's Harbour, Washington. At some point after 1894, the Fidalgo Island Packing Company purchased the vessel, outfitting and employing it as a cannery tender. It would have been active around the Southern Gulf Islands and Puget Sound. Henry Bell-Irving designed the company as a satellite to his Vancouver-based Anglo British Columbia Packing Company, and both operations were very successful. *Chehalis* changed owners again in 1916, when Seattle's Carey Davis Tug and Barge Company purchased it. Along with the tugs *Equator* and *Oregon*, *Chehalis* steamed countless nautical miles throughout Washington and British Columbia in the employ of Carey Davis.

Chehalis sailed from Seattle on 11 September 1921 for Canadian waters, but grounded on a reef near the entrance to Ladysmith Harbour early on the morning of 13 September. At the time of the grounding, John Finn, an American citizen, was master, while George R. Carey of the Carey Tug and Barge Company owned the vessel, according to documents from the American Department of Commerce. Carey dispatched a second company tug, *Oregon*, to provide assistance. The crew onboard *Chehalis* escaped without injuries.

Following the grounding, Canadian customs documents record the changing of *Chehalis*'s ownership and nationality. They state that *Chehalis* "stranded on a reef 5 miles from Chemainus and purchased in that condition by L. B. Noel. Floated and tied to wharf when appraised." Little

is known of Noel, other than that he had the papers of a Master Mariner and hailed from faraway Harbour Grace, Newfoundland. Noel paid $2,000 for *Chehalis*, and re-registered it as a Canadian vessel. Noel mostly used it for towing log booms, and never overhauled the engineering plant or accommodations for steam or electricity – it burned coal and relied on oil lamps until its loss forty-two years after its launch.

Loss

On 27 July 1932, Victoria's *Daily Colonist* recorded that "fire swept through the tug *Chehalis* yesterday afternoon and burned it to the water's edge as it lay moored off Arbutus Point waiting for a favorable tide," in order to navigate south through Samsun Narrows for Sidney with a log boom. The vessel had taken a large boom in tow at Mud Bay, and intended to deliver it to the Sidney Lumber Company.

Chehalis propeller at Maple Bay Marina, photo courtesy of Cam Campbell.

Chief Engineer C. Rafflaub first noticed the fire, which originated in the engine room around 14:00, and reported it to Captain Schade. The two men then woke three sleeping crewmen, and all onboard made a hasty escape after

gathering their belongings. The crew managed to escape in a lifeboat "after making a line from the log boom fast ashore," and landed at Maple Bay. The escape couldn't have been a moment too soon, as Schade reported that "within five minutes the tug was almost one mass of flames." At this point "Captain Schade immediately telephoned Captain Noel," who promptly left Victoria for the scene of the wreck. The Island Tug and Barge Company dispatched a tug to retrieve the boom, but *Chehalis* itself disappeared below the waterline shortly after burning. Sources do not record the salvage, and the tug vanishes from the historical record immediately following its loss.

Salvage

As stated above, no official record of salvage could be found. However, the absence of machinery and boiler on site suggests that salvers worked the tug at some point.

According to Mike Wright at the Maple Bay Marina, he was one of the people who raised the prop and shaft with the help of divers in the 1970s. They used a barge and winch to lift the prop and shaft and transport them to Birds Eye Cove where they are on display at the Maple Bay Marina.

Search and Discovery

The UASBC did not search for the *Chehalis* during its 1980-82 Gulf Islands project.

The UASBC's first attempt to relocate the wreck occurred on 25 March 2012. Jacques Marc recalled diving the wreck in the late 1970s. He also recalled it being in the upper Sansum Narrows, under the power line that crosses from Salt Spring Island to Vancouver Island, and that the hull was in shallow water. Based on this information, divers entered the water beneath the power line at 300-m intervals along the shore and swam south towards Arbutus Point, which marks the north entrance to Maple Bay. Despite covering the 20-foot bottom contour from the power line to Arbutus Point, the divers found no wreckage.

The UASBC began a second search after a tip from member Paul Spencer. He was reading an old issue of the UASBC *Foghorn* newsletter and learned that that Fred Rogers had actually written an article on the loss of the *Chehalis*. The article included a chart with the wreck location clearly marked.

Armed with Fred's chart, we tried another search 14 October 2012. The six-person team was spit up into three groups and dropped off a few hundred meters apart along the shore in the vicinity of the mark on the chart. Within ten minutes, divers were finding bits and pieces of wood and metal debris from the wreck. A short time later, the divers found the wreck site. Unfortunately, it was not a large intact site, but rather a scattering of some wood and metal pieces. The rudder was the largest extant piece on site. Additional parts like steel through-deck manhole covers, a boiler feed pump assembly, the engine room gong, a mooring bit, and multiple small brass valves were the only other parts found on site.

After the first dive, the team made an accurate GPS fix. The wreck is located 1.6 km north of Arbutus Point at 48° 50.157' N by 123° 35.404' W. It lies in 20-30 feet of water on a 9.8-foot tide.

During a second dive, divers made an underwater drawing of the rudder. It measured 1.8 m long by 1.2 m wide and was made of steel. One team swam to deeper water in search of the boiler, which may have rolled down slope. Despite successive passes across the path of the debris trail into the depths, divers discovered no larger items.

The site was revisited a third time on 10 November 2018. The goal of this dive was to confirm that nothing had been missed in previous dives. Divers searched to the east and west of the site and out into 60 feet of water but discovered nothing new.

Status

There is very little left of the *Chehalis*. There are just enough artifacts to confirm where it sank. The few artifacts present are not compelling and do not make this an attractive dive site.

Conclusions & Recommendations

This site is seldom visited and there isn't much left to explore. The UASBC therefore does not have any recommendations. The few remaining artifacts are protected by the *Heritage Conservation Act*.

References

BC Archives, GR 1237, Box 10, File 39. Canada Department of Transport, 13/1921, *Chehalis*, United States of America Department of Commerce Bureau of Navigation, Bill of Sale of Registered Vessel, 16 September 1921.

BC Archives, GR 1237, Box 10, File 39. Canada Department of Transport, 13/1921, *Chehalis*, Customs Canada – Entry for Home Consumption, 16 September 1921.

BC Archives, GR 1237, Box 10, File 39. Canada Department of Transport, 13/1921, *Chehalis*, Certificate of Survey, 18 October 1921.

BC Archives, GR 1237, Box 10, File 39. Canada Department of Transport, 13/1921, *Chehalis*, Application of Ownership by Individual, 22 October 1921.

Daily British Colonist, 17 September 1921.

Ibid., 27 July 1932.

List of Shipping Casualties Resulting in Total Loss in British Columbia and Coastal Waters Since 1897, (Transportation Safety Board of Canada, 1980).

National Archives, Master Carpenter's Certificates, 1865-1963, 642256 (Seattle). Chehalis County (became Gray's Harbor County) in 1915.

Newell, Gordon, ed. *The H. W. McCurdy Marine History of the Pacific Northwest: 1895-1965*, (Seattle: Superior Publishing Co., 1963), 265.

Newell, Dianne, ed. *Development of the Pacific Salmon-Canning Industry: A Grown Man's Game*, (Montreal: McGill–Queen's University Press 1989), 81.

Rogers, Fred. "Old Tug *Chehalis* Ended in Smoke and Flames." *Foghorn* Vol. 13, No. 6 (2002), 4.

Rogers, Fred. *More Shipwrecks of British Columbia* (Vancouver: Douglas & McIntyre., 1992), 62-63.

Searchable Vessels Database "Chehalis," https://www.nauticapedia.ca/dbase/Query/Shiplist5.php?id=25505

Mike Wright, personal communication with Fred Rogers, 12 July 2002.

Bill of Sale of Registered Vessel, (United States of America Department of Commerce Bureau of Navigation, 16 September 1921).

Clipper Ship *Cowper*

Clipper ship *Cowper* entering Hong Kong circa 1860, courtesy of Vallejo Gallery.

Official Number: Not issued before 1866

Registry: United States

Construction

Although *Cowper* is not referenced in any list of New England clippers, several contemporary newspaper accounts cite it as such through arrival and clearance notifications. The *Monthly Nautical Magazine* of 1855 lists it as ship-rigged at the time of its launch. However, information on its construction is conspicuously absent.

Pioneer shipbuilder Joshua Magoun built *Cowper* at his shipyard in Charleston, a suburb of Boston, in 1845. Magoun used oak fastened with copper and iron and designed the vessel as a two-decked vessel. It was ship-rigged, 181 ½ feet long, 34 ¾ feet wide and 24 feet deep. At the time of *Cowper's* launch, Magoun gave the

registered tonnage as 1024, while he gave the draft (presumably empty) as 24 feet. Based on an 1868 newspaper advertisement, historians know that it had accommodation for a few cabins and passengers, and was 7 feet 6 inches between decks. Chandlers metalled the hull in 1858 and again in May 1860, December 1862, November 1865, and December 1866.

Magoun built *Cowper* for well-known ship owners and operators Alpheus Hardy & Company of Boston. They owned two other J. Magoun-built ships, *Mountain Wave* (1852) and *Ocean Pearl* (1853). The *American Lloyd's Register of American & Foreign Shipping* confirms that the Hardys owned *Cowper* and that they had registered the vessel in Boston from 1854 until early 1869. The vessel is thought to have been named after the English poet William Cowper.

Operational History

Cowper had a far-reaching and distinguished sixteen-year career as a freighter. It initially operated out of Boston, and by the late 1850s ran out of San Francisco. Over the course of its career, the vessel visited ports in England, Ireland, Peru, Hong Kong, Australia, and Canada. Some highlights of its numerous voyages are summarized below.

Cowper sailed on its maiden voyage on 24 May 1854 from Boston. The vessel's new owners dispatched it to Callao, Peru, to load guano. The *Cowper* arrived on 31 September 1854 after a transit of one hundred days. It completed a second guano voyage in 1857, arriving back at Hampton Roads, Virginia, on 23 March 1858 after a ninety-day passage. *Cowper* completed a third voyage to Callao in 1863.

Cowper made its first appearance on the West Coast after arriving in San Francisco on 2 July 1857, 134 days from New York, laden with merchandise for D Gibb & Company. It returned to San Francisco a little over a year later on 13 November 1858, travelling 160 days from New York with cargo for Crosby & Libblee. While alongside the Vallejo Street Wharf in San Francisco on 4 December 1858, a winter storm drove *Cowper* against the jetty and damaged its bulwarks.

In 1859 *Cowper* travelled to Asia. It arrived back in San Francisco after a sixty-day transit from Hong Kong on 3 July 1860, carrying 426 Chinese passengers and 300 tons of produce. *Cowper* made a second trip to Hong Kong in 1868. It was reported departing Hong Kong for San Francisco on 19 May 1868 with cargo valued at $15,000.

On 11 September 1860, *Cowper* departed San Francisco for Cork (Queenstown) Ireland, arriving on 23 January 1861. The cargo was 1400 tons of prime wheat and 300 bales of wool. *Cowper* made a second trip from San Francisco to Cork on 18 August 1866.

Cowper probably entered the coal trade in 1865. On 10 December 1865, it was reported clearing Dartmouth,

England, for San Francisco with coal from Shields. It arrived in San Francisco on 14 May 1866 after a 160-day transit from Shields with coal for Stevens, Baker & Company.

On 5 August 1868, *Cowper* departed San Francisco for Sydney, Australia, with 30,267 sacks of wheat valued at $60,533, arriving 23 October 1868.

FOR SAN FRANCISCO direct.—The A 1 American clipper ship COWPER, 1500 tons, T. Sparrow, commander, will be dispatched on or about the 3rd December; has superior accommodation for a few cabin and intermediate passengers, being over 7 feet 6 inches between decks. Intending passengers are invited to inspect the ship, at Campbell's Wharf. Early application is necessary to secure berths, many being already engaged.

Apply to H. H. HALL, U. S. Consul, 21, Bridge-street.

Advertisement, *Sydney Morning Herald*, Saturday, 28 November 1868.

Cowper departed Sydney on 14 December 1868 with a load of coal, heading back to San Francisco. It arrived on 3 March 1869 (eighty days en route) with coal for Williams Blanchard & Company.

Hardy & Company sold *Cowper* to Rosenfeld & Birmingham on 4 April 1869. The vessel departed San Francisco for Nanaimo six days later. According to Victoria's *Daily Colonist*, the new owners purchased *Cowper* specifically for the coal trade. On 16 April 1869, it loaded coal at Nanaimo, returning to San Francisco on 24 April 1869.

Cowper maintained a schedule of a monthly round trip between San Francisco and Nanaimo until its wrecking, for a total of seven trips.

Loss

On the afternoon of Saturday, 20 November 1869, the government steamer *Sir James Douglas* took *Cowper* under tow, laden with 1,614 tons of coal. Once they cleared Nanaimo Harbour, the *Douglas* slipped *Cowper*.

Cowper set its sails and began its routine voyage for San Francisco. At 07:20 the following morning, the ship ran aground on a reef at the northwest corner of Tumbo Island. It struck heavily, bumped twice and then settled down on the rock. The crew made every effort to free the ship. They started the pumps but found that *Cowper* took on water freely. Regardless, they manned the pumps into Sunday evening. By 08:00 on Monday, the water in the hold had increased to 7 feet. The captain and four men set out in the ship's boat for Victoria to seek assistance.

After an exhausting journey, they arrived in Victoria at 17:30 on the same day. Captain Peck immediately stated his case to Captain Lyons, a senior officer of the Royal Navy Fleet at Esquimalt. Lyons orders the gunboat HMS *Boxer*, with a robust complement of sailors under Captain Egerton, to the wreck to render assistance.

Boxer sailed for the wrecked ship at 07:00 on Tuesday, 23 November, and remained anchored off the wreck after arriving. The salvage party conducted as thorough an examination as the condition of the ship would allow. They found that the tide ebbed and flowed through the broken planks and that they could only save the stricken vessel with the most favorable weather and by using pontoons. *Boxer* returned to Esquimalt on Wednesday, 25 November. Captain Peck remained behind with his ship to supervise salvage efforts.

Salvage

Captain Peck began the removal of the standing rigging from *Cowper*, which the crew loaded onto to the schooner *Alert*. He also proposed throwing overboard 600 tons of coal, intending to lighten and thus refloat the ship. If successful, he planned to tow *Cowper* back to Nanaimo for repairs.

On Thursday, 25 November, the Hudson's Bay Company steamer SS *Enterprise* sailed out to the wreck. Victoria's *Daily Colonist* reported a rumour that Rosenfeld & Birmingham had not insured *Cowper*, but that the cargo valued at $55,000 had been insured. The same paper also stated that those in seafaring circles held little hope that the vessel could be saved, and that interested parties had begun preparations for removing the cargo of coal.

On the morning of 26 November, the schooner *Alert* arrived in Victoria from the wreck, bringing a full cargo of sails, blocks, and standing rigging. Captain Peck was

reportedly still engaged in dismantling the ship and would fill Captain McKay's schooner *Favourite* with the remainder of the loose gear. The ship and cargo were to be sold at auction – the ship on account of the owners and the cargo on the account of the underwriters.

Captain Peck arrived in Victoria aboard the schooner *Favorite* on Saturday, 27 November. He had loaded the vessel with anchors, chains, ropes, sails, yards, and other appurtenances of the unfortunate ship. He informed the *Daily Colonist* that the rock his ship struck had not been charted by the authorities. He also reported that he had stripped *Cowper* to the lower and topsail yards, which still stood, and that he left it in charge of the officers and one seaman.

The *Cowper* and its cargo of coal were sold at auction on Wednesday 1 December 1869 by Mr. J. P. Davies & Company. R. Broderick bought the ship for $250 and the cargo for $575. The savaged goods were also sold.

Broderick dispatched the schooner *Discovery* to continue salvage work on the wreck. It returned to Victoria on 7 December with 45 tons of coal as well as rigging. Broderick and other salvagers still hoped to refloat the wreck.

The Saturday, 18 December edition of the *Daily Colonist* reported that the new owner would abandon *Cowper* as the slim possibility of refloating the vessel didn't warrant the expense likely to be incurred. Broderick sent a party to strip the copper off the ship's bottom.

The 21 December edition of the *Daily Colonist* reported that *Cowper* had disappeared from the rock on Friday, 17 December during a heavy nor'wester. The *Enterprise* passed the spot and could see no sign of the *Cowper*. The paper also reported that salvagers had saved 300 tons of coal.

In early April 1870, large sections of the *Cowper* were reportedly found on San Juan Island and on Friday Island.

No further information could be found on its disposition.

Search and Discovery

The UASBC attempted its first search for this wreck on 13 April 2019, but cancelled the dive because of high winds.

A second attempt to search for the *Cowper* occurred 14 September 2019. This time the weather cooperated and the search covered a portion of the reef system north of Pine Islet.

UASBC members carried out multiple dives. Team 1 started at coordinates 48° 48.346' N by 123° 06.986' W and swam southeast with the ebbing tide, for 800-850 m, covering the top and west side of the reef for 850 m, exiting at 48° 48.174' N by 123° 06.337' W. The bottom was found to be smooth rock that was relatively flat in the shallows but then dropped away steeply. The divers searched to a maximum depth of 65 feet (20 m). During their transit, Paul Spencer found a single 33-inch long steel bolt with nuts on either end concreted to the top of the reef in 25 feet of water. Nothing else was found.

Team 2 started just off shore of Pine Islet at 48° 48.106' N by 123° 05.682' W, and using scooters travelled 1.47 km northwest on a bearing of 287° and ended at 48° 48.338' N by 123° 06.828' W. The reef was found to be steeply sloping sandstone, which levelled out at about 60 feet (18 m). The scooter team transited at this depth and found a small 1.2-1.5 m long admiralty-type anchor with chain attached at 48° 48.241' N by 123° 06.422' W. To the east, the team found scattered fragments of some steel cable but nothing else.

These two searches covered the eastern reef system. A third dive looked at the western or inshore reef system. On this dive, two divers swam southeast into a strong flood (northwesterly) current and were unable to fulfill their objective. A third diver started at 48° 48.199' N by 123 07.141' W and drifted with the current for 600 m along the inner reef as deep as 67 feet (20 m) and exited at 48° 48.303' N by 123° 07.600' W. Nothing was found on this search.

Small anchor found during Cowper search. Photo courtesy of Ewan Anderson.

Status

The wreck of the *Cowper* remains undiscovered.

Conclusions and Recommendations

Additional searches should be carried out to try find *Cowper* so that the wreck's status can be assessed.

References

American Lloyd's Register of American & Foreign Shipping, 1859-1869.

http://library.mysticseaport.org/initiative/SPSearch. cfm?ID=617002

Bangor Daily Whig and Courier, 17 May 1866.

Boston Post, 1 September 1855.

Daily Alta California, 14 November 1858.

Ibid., 3 July 1860.

Ibid., 11 September 1860.

Ibid., 23 January 1866.

Ibid., 15 May 1866.

Ibid., 12 June 1866.

Ibid., 5 August 1868.

Ibid., 25 January 1869.

Ibid., 4 March 1869.

Ibid., 11 April 1869.

Ibid., 22 July 1869.

Ibid., 24 November 1869.

Freemans Journal, 24 January 1861.

New England Farmer, 27 May 1854.

Richmond Dispatch, 24 March 1858.

Rogers, Fred. *More Shipwrecks of British Columbia* (Vancouver: Douglas & McIntyre , 1992), 153.

Sacramento Daily Union, 9 April 1869.

San Francisco Chronicle, 4 April 1869.

Sydney Morning Herald, 27 November 1868.

Ibid., 28 November 1868.

Ibid., 5 December 1868.

The Monthly Nautical Magazine and Quarterly Review, Vol. 1 (1855), 302.

Times Picayune, 24 February 1863.

Victoria Daily British Colonist, August 18, 1866.

Ibid., 5 May 1869.

Ibid., 11 May 1869.

Ibid., 3 July 1869.

Ibid., 15 July 1869.

Ibid., 22 October 1869.

Sidewheel Steamer *Del Norte*

The *Princess Louise* was similar in size and rig to *Del Norte*. Image A-00114 courtesy of the Royal BC Museum and Archives.

Official Number: 6515

Signal Letters: JCBG

Registry: United States

Construction

Pioneer west-coast shipbuilder Henry Owens built the sidewheel paddle steamer SS *Del Norte* at the request of the California, Oregon and Mexico Steamship Company for their Holladay Line in 1864. The keel was laid 8 September 1864 and the vessel was launched at 09:00 on 10 December 1864, christened by Lizzie Foley.

The *Del Norte* was first steamship to be built in San Francisco. Owens used White oak and pine during the vessel's construction in his yard at Potrero (present-day San Francisco). He fastened the hull with copper below the waterline and iron above. *Del Norte* was 200 feet long, had a 30-foot beam with a hold 17 feet deep. Its unladen draft was 9 feet at its deepest point. Owens outfitted *Del Norte* with a two-cylinder oscillating steam engine removed from the retired steamer *Republic*. Murray & Hazlehurst of Baltimore, Maryland, originally constructed the engine. Each cylinder measured 54 inches in diameter, had a stroke of 72 inches, and combined to produce 225 nominal hp. Coffee and Risdon of San Francisco produced the two low-pressure boilers, which measured 25 ½ by 8 ½ feet and produced 40 pounds pressure. On either side of the hull, connected to the engines by a heavy shaft, were the paddlewheels, each measuring 21 feet in diameter and containing 22 spokes. *Del Norte* had two decks and was schooner-rigged.

Victoria's *Daily Colonist* described the vessel as being a very fine specimen of ship architecture, constructed substantially and durably. Owens purpose-built *Del Norte* to run three trips a month between San Francisco, Crescent City and Humboldt Bay, and launched it on 10 December 1864.

Operational History

Del Norte ran primarily on routes north of San Francisco under Captains Johnson, Fauntleroy, and Windsor. In 1867 it sailed for a short time in the Coos Bay trade and in 1868 began sailing from San Francisco to Puget Sound, Victoria, and occasionally to Alaska.

The California, Oregon and Mexico Steamship Company employed *Del Norte* within weeks of its launch. The vessel's routine arrivals and departures from San Francisco are chronicled in the *Alta California* and *Sacramento Daily Union* newspapers. The *Daily Union* recorded one of its early arrivals at San Francisco from Humboldt Bay with 50 passengers on 11 May 1865. A month later, it arrived with more passengers and $9,000 in bullion.

Del Norte saw excitement early in its career on 30 July 1865, when the coastwise steamer *Brother Jonathan* struck an uncharted rock near Point St. George, off the coast of Crescent City, California, with the loss of 225 passengers and crewmen and a fortune in gold coins. The victims included Brigadier General George Wright, the Union Commander of the Department of the Pacific, and Major E. W. Eddy. Under Captain Henry Johnson, the *Del Norte* steamed to Crescent City to convey the survivors and a number of bodies to San Francisco. More than two months after the accident, the *Del Norte* arrived at San Francisco on 13 October 1865, carrying the bodies of the general and major.

The following year, the California, Oregon and Mexico Steamship Company formed into a joint stock company. Under the laws of New York, executive membership changed the company name to the Oregon, California and Mexico Steamship Company.

Victoria's *Daily Colonist* recorded that the steamship *Del Norte*, under Captain Johnson, arrived on the afternoon

of 22 March 1866 with 117 passengers, including thirty-three from New Westminster, British Columbia. *Del Norte* carried general cargo. The paper also commented that owing to high fares, the vessel did not ferry the anticipated number of passengers.

In its short career, the *Del Norte* suffered at least two mishaps. The first occurred on 7 January 1866 when it struck Rincon rock on approach to the Folsom Street wharf in San Francisco. Local newspapers reported that the vessel struck quite heavily but suffered little damage, aside from a few sheets of copper. Next, on Friday, 8 November 1867, the *Del Norte* shipped a heavy sea while coming over Humboldt Bar. This seriously damaged the uppers and carried away one of the wheelhouses. In the same incident, a barrel killed an unnamed seaman after striking him in the chest.

1865 advertisement *Sacramento Daily Union*.

From 16 July 1866 until fall 1867, most arrival and departure records show *Del Norte* travelling back and forth between San Francisco, Crescent City, and Humboldt Bay. In 1868 Victoria's *Daily Colonist* began recording *Del*

Norte more frequently in northern waters.

The *Del Norte*'s first visit to British Columbia in 1868 occurred on 18 February. The *Daily Colonist* reported that Captain Windsor arrived at 08:30 "after a very quick and pleasant trip from San Francisco. The *Del Norte* brings 60 passengers among who are several residents and a number of gentlemen who have come to join Her Majestie's [sic] fleet at Esquimalt." Later that year, on 15 September, the vessel departed San Francisco for Victoria, Port Townsend, Fort Tongas, and Wrangell, Alaska. *Del Norte* cleared San Francisco again on 25 September for Victoria, laden with a cargo valued at $52,740. On 29 September, *Del Norte* delivered troops to San Juan Island and Fort Wrangell before returning to Victoria en route to San Francisco.

Loss

Del Norte wrecked on a return trip to San Francisco from Sitka, Alaska, in October 1868.

It left Nanaimo, its final port of call, at 19:00 on Thursday, 22 October 1868, bound for Victoria via Porlier Pass. Sources report clear weather when *Del Norte* entered the pass at 09:00 on 23 October. However, not long after entering the pass, a dense fog enveloped the vessel. Captain Windsor, not thinking it prudent to proceed and not having room to turn his vessel around, began reversing into the Gulf of Georgia. During the manoeuvre, the current carried *Del Norte* stern-first onto Canoe Reef. The grounding initially caused superficial damage, including displacing the rudder and knocking away a portion of the false keel. Captain Windsor immediately had the coal moved forward to lighten the stern, the bow anchors run out into 18 fathoms of water, and the cables hauled taunt.

Del Norte remained fixed in this position until 02:00 the next morning. Low tide occurred shortly afterward, and with the stern well out of the water, *Del Norte* suddenly took a sheer over onto its starboard bilge, putting the forward guards underwater and breaking the sternpost. Captain Windsor was building a bulkhead to confine the water to the stern, but the rising tide rushed through the bottom of the vessel and drove out the men, halting their work. At daylight the crew ferried ashore passengers: Mr. W. K. Bull, his three children, a Sergeant Barr, and his wife

and three children. The crew also brought ashore all the ship's stores, furniture, and the crew's personal luggage.

In the interval, Captain Clarke of the government steamer *Sir James Douglas* received a message at Nanaimo to proceed to the wreck. Clarke complied immediately, but could not render any material assistance. *Del Norte* rapidly took on water, which by this point had reached the furnace doors. Mr. Turner (a passenger aboard the *Sir James Douglas*) believed that the potential disaster would result in the total loss of the vessel.

Drawing looking from Strait of Georgia into Porlier Pass showing *Del Norte* aground on Canoe Rock on the morning of 27 October 1868.

At some point Captain Windsor must have arranged for the steamer *Active* to ferry him and his crew to Victoria, as they arrived there on 27 October. Windsor left three men in charge of the wreck site, and the *Daily Colonist* reported that "there is no hope of the *Del Norte* being gotten off the rocks." The *Daily Colonist* further reported, "it is not even yet known whether an effort will be made by the owners, although instructions have been asked from San Francisco on that point."

Four days after Windsor and his men arrived in Victoria, the steamer *Emma* departed for the wreck site. The ship carried an expedition chartered by the Oregon, California and Mexico Steamship Company to investigate the condition of the wreck. The trusty *Colonist* relates that "it is said that the vessel can be gotten off the rock but the expense of doing so, together with the repairs would be only a little less than which a new vessel could be built. She lies precisely as she was left by Capt. Windsor, but even the removal of the boilers and her machinery would be expensive." About a week later, the *Emma* made another expedition to again assess the wreck, fearing further damage from a southeast gale.

It seems that a series of southeast gales lashed the Southern Gulf Islands, and that although the *Emma*'s second expedition discovered the *Del Norte* exactly as Captain Windsor had left it, the weather soon took its toll on the precariously balanced wreck. On the evening of 13 November, one of *Del Norte*'s mates arrived in Victoria and reported that "during a severe southeaster of Tuesday night the steamer slipped from the rock on which she struck and went down in 10 fathoms of water. On Wednesday morning not a vestige of the wreck was visible. All hope of raising the hull must now be abandoned." As it turns out, the Hudson's Bay Company's steamer *Otter* had been dispatched to "assist saving the wreck," but didn't arrive in time to be of service, and the mate reported that the gale would have prevented any seamanship work regardless. The *Otter* arrived at Victoria from Puget Sound on 16 November, reporting "terrific southeast gales for several days in the sound."

Salvage

No known commercial salvage occurred on the wreck aside from the removal of some fittings and furniture before the hull sank.

UASBC divers Larry McFarlane and Jeff Yallop on *Del Norte* site 1978. Photo courtesy of UASBC Collection.

Search and Discovery

Victoria-based sport divers Doug Hartley, Bob Zielinski, Eric Marles and Jim Goddard located *Del Norte* in early 1971. During their explorations the divers retrieved the following artifacts:

- two boiler sight glasses
- eight portholes
- two – 24-inch high crockery pickle jars
- sixteen Empire Soda bottles from San Francisco
- two whisky bottles
- one small anchor and
- several pieces of 30-inch diameter copper tubing.

The wreck location became known to the broader diving community in 1973 and quickly became a popular destination for exploration and souvenir hunting. At the time, legislation had not been passed outlawing the removal of artifacts from wrecks, so sport divers absconded with many of the small artifacts.

The UASBC visited the *Del Norte* for the first time on 17 and 18 July 1976 to carry out a preliminary investigation. The team completed fourteen dives on the site, completing a preliminary survey of the wreck that showed the location of the boilers, engine, and major artifacts. The group concluded that the UASBC should conduct further research and survey work on the wreck, and also that steps should be taken to protect the site.

The UASBC urged the BC government to designate the *Del Norte* a protected heritage site. Such a designation would make it an offence under the *Heritage Conservation Act* to remove, tamper with, or disturb the wreck. Unfortunately, the provincial government did not act on the recommendation and over the ensuing years diving activity on the *Del Norte* intensified. The wreck continued to be disturbed and artifacts removed.

In 1978 the UASBC placed an educational plaque on the wreck that detailed the *Del Norte*'s dimensions, construction, and circumstances of its loss. The plaque also urged divers to "Please Respect Your Maritime Heritage." Divers responded to the plaque phenomenally. The UASBC noted a noticeable decline in artifact removal and disturbance of the wreck as the diving community became aware of its importance.

During the survey of Gulf Island shipwrecks, UASBC divers visited *Del Norte* on 12 and 13 December 1981 and became concerned about how boat anchors were damaging the wreck's boilers. In response, the UASBC applied to the BC Heritage Trust in 1982 for funds to install a mooring buoy on site. The BC Heritage Trust turned down the initial application, but funded the project in early 1984. In March 1984, UASBC installed a mooring buoy to protect the wreck from anchor damage. The UASBC maintained the buoy on the site until 1998, after the loss of five different buoys and the evolution of the GPS.

Status

The UASBC dived on the *Del Norte* five times during its re-inventory of Southern Gulf Island wrecks.

The wreck lies in an exposed location on the inside of Canoe Islet and is subject to the currents that pass through Porlier Pass. The wreck lies at coordinates 49° 01.594' N by 123° 35.292' W. To examine the wreck, all dives were completed at slack water, which lasts 35-45 minutes on average. The UASBC spent 34 person-dives doing a datum offset survey on the wreck. However, UASBC member Ewan Anderson undertook a photogrammetry project on the site, which provided better documentation. As a result of Ewan's work, a 3D model was produced for the site, enabling us to examine the wreck from various angles.

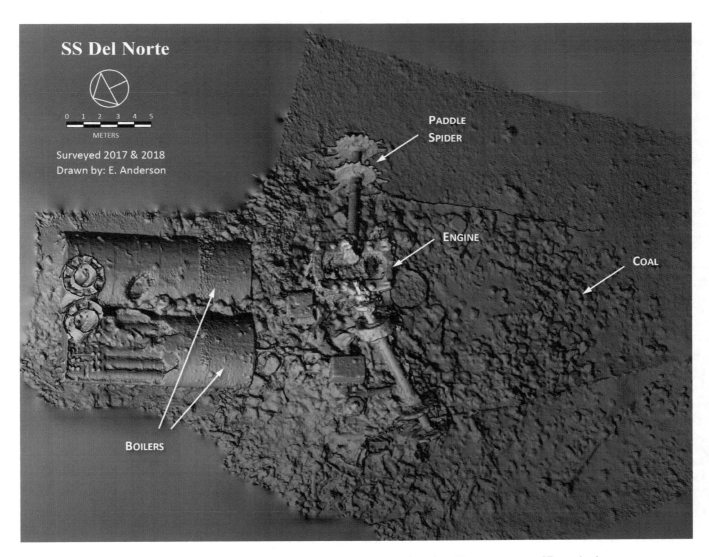

Photogrammetric model of *Del Norte* boilers, paddle spiders and engine. Photo courtesy of Ewan Anderson.

The remains of the vessel lie on a sloping sand-shell bottom, oriented along a 018° heading stern to bow in 40-90 feet of water. A substantial portion of the vessel remains on site, including remnants of the wooden hull, the engine, two boilers, and the paddle wheel shafts and spiders. As is evident in the site plan, the port side boiler is heavily damaged. The outer steel shell has collapsed, leaving a gaping hole for two thirds of its length. Careless anchoring caused the initial damage, and corrosion and structural fatigue has done the rest. The starboard boiler is more intact, but is fragile and already has several holes in it.

The oscillating engine is of particular interest. The *Del Norte* was reported to be equipped with a two-cylinder oscillating steam engine removed from the retired steamer *Republic*. We could not find any drawings of the original *Republic* oscillating engine of the 1849. However, Bob Sheret, in his book *Smoke Ash and Steam*, describes their operation:

> On an oscillating engine the cylinders oscillate back and forth doing away with the necessity of connecting rods. The cylinders were not fixed, as with most steam engines, but oscillated on their centers eliminating the need for connecting rods. The cylinders could be placed directly underneath the crankshaft or at an angle to reduce engine height. Each cylinder was mounted on trunnions. The trunnions were placed in the middle of the cylinder so that they could swing or oscillate. Steam was let in and out of the cylinders by hollow trunnions. Valves located on the cylinders were operated by eccentrics.

During our investigation of the wreck site, we only found one cylinder directly beneath the crankshaft with a connecting rod protruding from the top. Aft of the engine framework is a second upright cylindrical object. However, it has no framework associated with it and we could not locate a connecting rod within the wreckage. This raised the question: was the *Del Norte* equipped with a twin-cylinder engine?

Our conclusion is yes, the engine probably had two cylinders but that some components are missing. UASBC member Jiri Kotler, a retired engineer, pointed out that if the *Del Norte* had been powered with a single cylinder engine, it would have needed a large flywheel to prevent the engine stalling at top dead centre. We did not observe a large flywheel on site.

Conclusions and Recommendations

The *Del Norte* has significant scientific value because of its unique oscillating steam engine. The engine was originally built in 1849 for another ship, the SS *Republic*, and was the first such engine designed and built in the United States. More research is needed to determine how the *Del Norte* engine was constructed and how it may have worked. Knowing this information will help us identify what each of the engine components on site are, and what might be missing.

The survey dives observed that the UASBC's educational plaque was deteriorating. It should be replaced in the next two years.

References

American Lloyd's Register of American and Foreign Shipping, 1866.

https://research.mysticseaport.org/item/l017595/l017595-c017/

Kemble, John H. *Panama Route 1848-1869*, (New York: Da Capo Press, 1972).

Lawson, Will. *Pacific Steamers*, (Glasgow: Brown, Son & Ferguson Ltd., 1975).

Otis, Fessenden Nott. *Isthmus of Panama: History of the Panama Railroad 1867*, (Whitefish: Kessinger Publishing, LLC, 2010), 225-226.

Rogers, Fred. *Historic Divers of British Columbia – A History of Hardhat Diving, Salvage and Underwater Construction*, (Duncan: Firgrove Publishing, 2003).

Sacramento Daily Union, Vol. 28, No. 4283, 13 December, 1864.

Ibid., Vol. 28, No. 4284, 14 December 1864.

Ibid., Vol. 29, No. 4412, 12 May 1865.

Ibid., Vol. 29, No. 4438, 12 June 1865.

Ibid., Vol. 29, No. 4463, 12 July 1865.

Ibid., Vol. 29, No. 4477, 28 July 1865.

Ibid., Vol. 29, No. 4503, 28 August 1865.

Ibid., Vol. 29, No. 4488, 10 August 1865.

Ibid., Vol. 30, No. 4581, 27 November 1865.

Ibid., Vol. 30, No. 4616, 8 January 1866.

Ibid., Vol. 31, No. 4774, 17 July 1866.

Ibid., Vol. 31, No. 4784, 28 July 1866.

Ibid., Vol. 32, No. 4838, 29 September 1866.

Ibid., Vol. 32, No. 4864, 30 October 1866.

Ibid., Vol. 33, No. 5006, 15 April 1867.

Ibid., Vol. 33, No. 5022, 2 May 1867.

Ibid., Vol. 34, No. 5190, 15 November 1867.

Ibid., Vol. 34, No. 5190, 15 November 1867.

Ibid., Vol. 33, No. 5047, 31 May 1867.

Ibid., Vol. 33, No. 5084, 15 July 1867.

Ibid., Vol. 34, No. 5260, 6 February 1868.

Ibid., Vol. 35, No. 5300, 24 March 1868.

Ibid., Vol. 36, No. 5460, 25 September 1868.

Ibid., Vol. 36, No. 5487, 27 October 1868.

Santa Cruz Weekly Sentinel, Vol. 9, No. 30, 31 December, 1864..

The Daily British Colonist, January 19, 1965.

Ibid., March 23, 1866.

Ibid., December 20, 1865.

Ibid., February 3, 1868.

Ibid., February 19, 1868.

Ibid., September 29, 1868.

Ibid., October 14, 1868.

Ibid., October 24, 1868.

Ibid., October 26, 1868.

Ibid., November 2, 1868.

Ibid., November 12, 1868.

Ibid., November 14, 1868.

Ibid., November 17, 1868.

Ibid., October 26, 1918.

Ibid., September 11, 1938.

Wildman, Rounsevelle. "Evolution of Shipping and Ship Building in California." *Overland Monthly*, (1895), 285-292.

Wright, E. W., ed. *Lewis & Dryden's Marine History of the Pacific Northwest*, (New York: Antiquarian Press Ltd., 1961), 137.

Steamer *Emily Harris*

Emily Harris at Sooke Image g-00356 courtesy of the Royal BC Museum and Archives.

Official Number: None (predates official numbers)

Registry: Canada

Construction

Shipbuilder Peter Holmes built the *Emily Harris* in his Victoria yard in late 1860, and launched it on 3 January 1861 on the order of Victoria's Messrs. Harris, Carrol & Co. The first steamer of exclusively British Columbian origin, Holmes also fitted the hull with a propeller, another first on the coast. The *Daily British Colonist* recorded the dimensions as "100 feet in length, 16 feet of beam and 6 feet, 6 inches depth of hold." A surviving archival sketch of the *Emily Harris* supports that it was schooner-rigged on masts fore and aft and had a small cabin amidships. Holmes supposedly modelled the vessel after an Aboriginal canoe, desiring a deeper draft and the capability to weather rugged coastal conditions by using reinforced timbers of live oak.

One "Mr. Dougal" manufactured the vessel's engines in his Victoria foundry alongside a "Mr. Allen," who would become the ship's first engineer. The launch notice extolled the engines and machinery, announcing, "they will be 30 horsepower, and have 12 inch cylinders and an 18 inch stroke. The screw is four feet six inches in diameter, 17 inches long. The boiler, which is tubular, was built at Watson's machine shop . . . It has been tested with hydraulic power and withstood a pressure of 140 pounds." The *Emily Harris* could accommodate fifteen passengers in cabins "fitted up in a neat manner" and eighty tons of freight.

Operational History

The *Emily Harris* quickly became a workhorse of early British Columbian shipping, typically plying the waters around the Southern Gulf Islands and frequently loading coal at Nanaimo. Over 1861 and 1862, it made numerous trips to New Westminster and various ports between Victoria and Nanaimo under Captain Court. Impressively, the *Emily Harris* successfully ferried members of the Eureka Copper Company to the Stikine River and northwest coast of British Columbia over the summers of 1862 and 1863, formidable journeys even today. When it wasn't destined for uncharted territory laden with adventurous gold prospectors, the vessel called at secondary ports like Comox, Olympia, Bentinck Arm, and Port Moody.

In the vessel's early years, it had various captains – for example, in 1863 Captain Hewitt and Captain McIntosh were in command at different times, and in 1862 a Captain Lawson took the vessel to the Northwest coast, while Captains Chambers and Gardener also occasionally took command.

In 1864 the vessel solely engaged in local transport and jobbing under the command of Captains McIntosh and Chambers. Frequent complaints that the *Emily Harris* would deliver mail up to ten days late suggest that it had difficulty maintaining its schedules. Evidently the vessel was dependable enough to be almost constantly at sea, and made yet another major voyage to the Queen Charlotte Islands (present-day Haida Gwaii) in May 1865.

Captain Frain, the *Emily Harris*'s longest-serving skipper, took command in January 1866. That year, advertisements extolled the vessel "having been thoroughly overhauled and refitted in hull and machinery, and her propelling power increased." During the summer of 1866, government authorities outfitted the *Emily Harris* with unspecified armaments during the Fenian raids, and in October of the following year it sank near Trial Island, only to be refloated by Frain, somehow having sustained "little or no damage."

In January 1868, the *Emily Harris* underwent repairs in Laing's Yard in Victoria, and in 1869 Frain turned over with Captain Greenwood. Unfortunately, Greenwood died onboard of a heart attack on 12 July 1869, prompting Frain to resume and retain command until the vessel's mysterious loss in 1871.

Loss

On the evening of 14 August 1871, the *Emily Harris* sank after experiencing an apparent boiler explosion. The ill-fated steamer loaded sixty tons of coal and other freight at Nanaimo consigned to Broderick & Company, and began its southbound transit for Victoria. The ship's complement on that voyage consisted of the veteran Captain Frain, a cook, an engineer, one passenger, and three Aboriginal people.

According to survivors' testimony, at 20:30 on 14 August 1871, an explosion tore through the *Emily Harris*. Survivors claimed it happened in Trincomali Channel somewhere between Salt Spring and Galiano Islands, possibly between Fernwood and Walker Hook. The vessel sank after drifting for around thirty minutes, and the engineer and three Aboriginals swam to Salt Spring Island's shore, while Captain Frain, the cook, and a male passenger either drowned or succumbed to injuries sustained in the blast.

The following morning, the survivors arrived at the residence of Salt Spring Island's constable, Henry Sampson, who escorted the four men to Vesuvius Bay where he knew he could hail the *Sir James Douglas*. After delivering the men to the *Sir James Douglas*, Sampson returned to his home at Beggs Settlement. With the help of two other men, he began a two-day search of the shorelines of Prevost Island, Long Harbour, Captain's Pass, and Walker Hook, to no avail.

The *Sir James Douglas* embarked the four survivors and ferried them to Nanaimo. En route they provided statements to Captain Clarke, the vessel's skipper, who considered their testimonies contradictory and therefore suspect. Clarke "concluded to send the Indians to prison," and probably confined them onboard while overnight at Nanaimo.

Upon arrival back in Victoria, the engineer immediately jumped overboard and fled, while two of the Aboriginal people entered police custody and the third seems to have spent time recovering from extensive scalding. One "Inspector Bowden" later located the engineer, who explained that fright caused him to flee, but that he had since composed himself and agreed to assist in the investigation – one could reasonably assume that the engineer may have been able to prevent the explosion, a possibility which may have induced his flight.

On Friday, 18 August, Victoria's Lieutenant-Governor Trutch dispatched the *Sir James Douglas* to search the suspected region of the disaster. The *Sir James Douglas* succeeded in locating two doors and a barrel, but did not locate any survivors, a debris field, or anything that might hint at exactly where the *Emily Harris* sank. Victoria's citizenry immediately assumed foul play, although such accusations likely had racial motivation. Further, the fate of the survivors is unknown and they do not appear to have faced charges.

Salvage

Mr. Copeland, an engineer, and four others started in a boat on the morning of Friday, 18 August to examine the potential scene and the prospect of raising the vessel. It must be assumed that they did not find the wreck as no salvage was ever reported.

Search and Discovery

Based on the survivors' statements, it is believed that the accident occurred in Trincomali Channel, on the northeast side of Salt Spring Island, about midway between Walker Hook and Captain's Pass. The width of the channel at this point is 2 miles (3.25 km). The distance to the Salt Spring Island shore from the middle of the channel would be about 0.75-1 mile.

Constable Sampson related that on the evening of Monday, 14 August, he saw the *Emily Harris* pass in the usual way and heard nothing of any explosion. Constable Sampson lived at Beggs Settlement (present-day Fernwood), so we know the *Emily Harris* was beyond Fernwood Point before it exploded. The four survivors said that after they abandoned ship, they swam for two miles to reach the Salt Spring Island shore. The four survivors arrived at Constable Sampson's place on Tuesday morning (time unknown) and reported that their boiler had burst.

Constable Sampson provided statements to Captain Clarke of the *Sir James Douglas* that the boiler exploded at 20:30 and that the vessel sank thirty minutes later. According to the Canadian Hydrographic Service, the tide was high at 18:00 on Monday, 14 August 1871 and the current would have been ebbing south at the time the accident happened. Charts show that the current runs at 1-2 knots in the channel. This means that the vessel would have drifted about one mile further south after exploding. The fact that the survivors walked back to Fernwood suggests that they reached shore before Nose Point. If we assume that they swam 1-2 miles diagonal with the current after the vessel sank, we can place the site of the sinking about midway between Walker Hook and Captain's Pass.

The waters of Trincomali Channel between Walker Hook and Captain's Pass average 20 fathoms (36 m) and do not exceed 24 fathoms (44 m). The bottom topography is relatively even, consisting of a sand-shell bottom. Due to the depths of the search area between Captain's Pass and Walker Hook, we considered conventional diver-style swim searches impractical – they would be imperfect at such depths, and would require hazardous decompression routines, not to mention the size of the search area, 8 km long by 1.5 km wide.

The UASBC first tried searching for *Emily Harris* on 10 October 1976. We had engaged renowned side-scan sonar expert Dr. Harold Edgerton to search for the wreck of the *Zephyr*. When that search was complete, we used the afternoon of 10 October to search Trincomali Channel for *Emily Harris*. Unfortunately, Edgerton located no promising targets.

The UASBC searched for the *Emily Harris* a second time in March 1982 during our first Gulf Islands project. At the time, the UASBC decided that the use of side-scan sonar equipment would be the most effective method of looking for the wreck. To this end, the UASBC approached Can-Dive Services of North Vancouver with the hope that they would donate the use of such a unit for the search. Can-Dive Services (Phil Nuytten) agreed to donate the use of a side-scan sonar unit, and operator Mark Atherton volunteered his time and expertise. We chartered the vessel MV *Oceaner* to serve as the survey platform and provide accommodation for expedition members.

On the weekend of 27-29 March 1982, the team deployed the sonar unit in Trincomali Channel at the entrance to Captain's Pass and towed at a speed of 1 knot parallel with the Salt Spring shore as far as Walker Hook. We kept constant checks on speed and position by consulting the radar, compass, and shoreline features. For twelve hours, we towed the sonar unit back and forth in Trincomali Channel, each sweep overlapping the previous one to make a complete survey of the sea floor.

The side-scan operations revealed only one target of interest. Divers checked the marked location and found it to be an uncharted rock outcropping about the same dimensions as the *Emily Harris*. The UASBC concluded that the *Emily Harris* may not be in the area that previous research identified as the likely wreck site.

In the late 1990s, the UASBC learned through Gary Grant of Campbell River that a Nanaimo seafood harvester, Brian Crawford, had found a porthole off the southwest side of Prevost Island while diving for urchins in the mid 1990s. The porthole was brought up by Crawford but his skipper told him to throw it back in. We speculated that it could be from the *Emily Harris*. The site is within the broad parameters of where the wreck might be if it had drifted further south before sinking, or if foul play was involved.

Based on this new lead, the society contacted Brian Crawford and arranged to take him out to the site. On 28 February 2004, the UASBC chartered the dive tender *Loup de Mer* from Rockfish Divers of Brentwood Bay and travelled to Prevost Island. Since it had been quite a while since Crawford had found the porthole, his memory of the exact location was a bit sketchy. We settled upon a few locations, primarily the points of land between Richardson Bay and Red Islets, and conducted a number of contour searches. The dives we made were unique. The shore was rock that gave way to sand at about 20 feet. The bottom was covered in more sea pens than we had seen before – literally hundreds, if not thousands, of them. Unfortunately, we were unable to come up with any further evidence pointing to the location of the *Emily Harris*.

On 17 May 2016, our dive on the *Zephyr* was cancelled due to bad weather. As a backup plan, we travelled to the northeast corner of Prevost Island and did a swim search from Peile Point to a point 1 km south (48 50 40.26N by 123 23 19.56 W), looking for evidence of the *Emily Harris*, without success.

On 19 February 2017, the UASBC again searched for the *Emily Harris*. Our goal was to search the inshore waters along the Salt Spring Island coastline from Nose Point north to Walker Hook. The rationale was that anything broken loose from the vessel during its sinking would have been carried south, potentially drifting ashore along the Salt Spring coastline.

To begin the search, we established four GPS way points (positions) 400 m apart, beginning at Nose Point and going north. On the day of the search the tide was ebbing, which meant the current was flowing south. Each buddy team was dropped on a way point and asked to swim south along the 30-40-foot depth contour.

When the first search was completed, we continued the search from four additional way points plotted to the north. The group swam 3.85 km of coastline from position 48° 52.229' N by 123° 27.801' W south to position 48° 50.955' N by 123° 25.342' W. We found the shoreline along Nose Point to be steep and rocky. This continued underwater to about 25-30 feet, after which the bottom became sand and shells. During the entire search, we found virtually no sign of human artifacts of any sort and nothing that could have come from the 1871 wreck of the *Emily Harris*.

Divers Holger Heitland & Ewan Anderson board *MV Cape Able* after searching the waters off Nose Point.

On 12 November 2017, the UASBC continued its swim search of the shallow waters off the east coast of Salt Spring Island. This time we started at the north end of Walker Hook and proceeded south. Divers were placed in the water at way points about 400 m apart, and again swam south. After completing our two dives , we had successfully searched between Walker Hook and Nose Point, covering 8.2 km of shoreline. We also dropped a scooter buddy team on Atkins Reef located 0.6 km off the east shore of Salt Spring Island. This team circumnavigated the reef but found no evidence of shipwreck debris.

In spring 2018, Jacques Marc contacted the Canadian Hydrographic Service (CHS) regarding potential charting work in Trincomali Channel, with the idea that the CHS might detect some unexplained anomalies during its charting operations. The CHS completed a survey in 2018 around Atkins Reef and Walter Hook to fill in the gap between Atkins Reef and Salt Spring Island, but nothing showed up in this area other than rocks. Patrick McNeill, a hydrographer with CHS, looked through the 2003 multi-beam data for Trincomali Channel and found only one feature that might be the right shape and size for *Emily Harris*. It was in 71 m of water off Nose Point at 48° 51 .229 N, 123° 25 .207 W. The Parks Canada Underwater Archaeology Service examined the coordinate area with their high-resolution multi-beam on 8 May 2019, but concluded that the feature was a rock.

On 28 May 2019, Craig Lessels, another hydrographer with CHS, advised Jacques Marc that CHS had finished processing the 2018 survey data for Trincomali Channel and he had identified a couple of potential targets. One target was the same one that Patrick McNeill had identified and had already been ruled out. The second target lies close to shore off Nose Point in 76 m (250 feet) of water at 48° 50 .987 N by 123° 25 .226 W. The features on the bottom strongly resemble topography but nonetheless will have to be checked out at some future date.

Status

The wreck of the *Emily Harris* remains undiscovered. The search for this important piece of BC's maritime heritage will have to wait until new clues or information comes to light.

Recommendations

None.

References

Griffiths, David W. *A Report on the Historic Shipwrecks of the Southern Gulf Islands of British Columbia.* (Vancouver, unpublished, 1982), 5-18.

Rogers, Fred. *Shipwrecks of British Columbia,* (Vancouver: J. J. Douglas Ltd., 1976), 68-69.

Spencer, Paul. "The Mystery of the *Emily Harris.*" *Foghorn,* Vol. 15, No. 3, (May 2004).

Item G-00346, Royal British Columbia Museum.

The Daily British Colonist, 4 January 1861

Ibid., 28 July 1862.

Ibid., 28 October 1863.

Ibid., 13 January 1866.

Ibid., 11 June 1866.

Ibid., 28 October 1867.

Ibid., 16 August 1871.

Ibid., 18 August 1871.

Ibid., 19 August 1871.

Ibid., 20 August 1871.

Wright, E. W., ed. *Lewis & Dryden's Marine History of the Pacific Northwest.* (New York: Antiquarian Press, Ltd., 1961), 98, 161, 198.

http://www.collectionscanada.gc.ca/obj/s4/f2/dsk3/ftp04/nq24350.pdf

Craig Lessels, email correspondence with J. Marc, 28 May, 2019.

Patrick McNeill, email correspondence with J. Marc. 3 April, 2019.

Tug *Henry Foss*

Henry Foss underway in Puget Sound, courtesy of Michael Skalley Collection.

Official Number: 774080

Signal Letters: KFWG

Construction

H. B. Kirby of Ballard Washington built and launched *Henry Foss* on 13 May 1900. L. H. Coolidge designed it as a cannery tender for Pacific American Fisheries of Bellingham. Built of wood, the vessel had a single deck, one mast and measured 100 feet overall, was 22 feet wide and 12 feet 3 inches deep. The gross tonnage was 122 and the net tonnage 79. At the time of its launch, a Vulcan compound steam engine provided propulsion. Its cylinders measured 13 and 28 inches in diameter and had a stroke of 24 inches. The engine generated 450 hp. Pacific American Fisheries named their new vessel *John Cudahy* after one of their biggest Chicago stockholders.

The construction cost $30,000.

The Foss Company purchased the *Cudahy* on 19 June 1941 and conducted extensive rebuilding. They renewed the hull framing, planking, deck beams and guards. Foss also removed the compound steam engine and replaced it with a 1,000-hp Enterprise diesel. Further, they constructed and installed a new deckhouse and pilot house. Foss launched the rebuilt vessel on 26 May 1942, re-christening it the *Henry Foss*. Henry Foss was the youngest of four children born to Norwegian immigrant parents, Andrew and Thea Foss, the first owners and operators of Foss Launch and Tug Company.

Operational History

Pacific American Fisheries employed the *Cudahy* as a cannery tender immediately after its launch, but in 1905 they determined that the tug was to big. The company sold *Cudahy* to Gray's Harbor Stevedoring Company of Aberdeen, Washington, for use as a support tug for vessels entering Gray's Harbor. It also acted as a pilot vessel.

In 1919 Grays Harbor Stevedoring sold *Cudahy* to the Merrill & Ring Logging Company for towing log rafts from the Pysht River log dump on the Straits of Juan de Fuca to Port Angeles. Three years later they sold the tug to Allman Hubble Tug Company of Hoquiam, Washington, who returned it to Gray's Harbor to serve as a bar tug. During its time with Hubble, *Cudahy* participated in several rescues, most notably saving the crew of the steam schooner *Caoba* in 1925. En route from Willapa Harbour to San Francisco, heavy seas opened up the hull of the unfortunate vessel and flooded the engine room. *Cudahy* responded to the distress call and proved instrumental in saving many of the crew.

In 1930 the Allman Hubble Tug Company sold *Cudahy* to Knappton Towboat Company for general towing on the Columbia River and Oregon coast. By the late 1930s, the tug had deteriorated to such an extent that Knappton laid the vessel up and tried to sell it on an as-is-where-is basis. The Foss Company recognized that the vessel still had some life left and bought the hull 19 June 1941. They had her towed to the Foss yard and *Cudahy* underwent a year-long rebuild. As detailed above, Foss re-launched the vessel with the new name *Henry Foss*.

Two weeks after the launch, the American government requisitioned the *Foss* for military duty in the Second World War, assigning it to the US Army Corps of Engineers. The tug served them for eighteen months, completing numerous barge runs to Alaska, after which the army returned it in good condition. After a brief refit, Foss put the tug into service towing log rafts between various Puget Sound destinations – but in 1944, tragedy struck.

The *Foss* left Tacoma with thirty-seven sections of logs bound for Port Angeles on 12 September 1944. Extreme weather forced the tug to anchor near Port Townsend on 14 September. Captain Carlsen, needing to make a phone call, boarded the tug workboat along with Mate Talbert and a deckhand, and headed for Port Townsend. On their return in the dark, the workboat flipped in rough seas, spilling all three men into the water. The captain and mate both drowned, leaving the deckhand as the sole survivor.

The *Foss* towed out of Port Angeles for most of its remaining years. Between 1956 and 1958, it supplemented the Seattle-based ocean-going tug fleet by making several voyages to southeastern and southwestern Alaska. In fall 1958, the tug returned to its Port Angeles service. Early in the evening of 12 February 1959, the *Foss* delivered a tow from Rayonier's log dump at Sekiu to Port Angeles and then retired to the Foss dock. After a crew change, the owners dispatched the *Foss* to Ladysmith, BC, to pick up a log tow for Port Angeles.

Loss

Foss left Port Angeles just before midnight on 12 February. As it crossed the Strait of Juan de Fuca, the weather worsened significantly. A fifty-knot gale, rain, and rough seas buffeted the stalwart tug. The weather remained bad as the *Foss* entered Haro Strait, steaming between Pender and Salt Spring Island.

Without warning, the tug ran hard aground on a rock at 04:00 13 February. The captain backed the tug off the rock, only to be met with disaster. Once free of the rock, the vessel quickly filled with water and sank. The seven crewmen had to abandon ship by launching the lifeboat and workboat. While the crew was trying to climb into the lifeboat, the tug took a sudden list causing the deck gear and mast to come crashing down alongside the two boats, swamping them. A minute later, *Foss* rolled completely over and sank, throwing all seven men into the cold rough water.

Although they all reached the overturned lifeboat and hung on, they slowly succumbed to hypothermia, and one by one they slipped below the surface. Two held on until rescued, but only one survived and continued to work for the company for the following forty years. The loss of six men was a tragic event for the Foss Company.

Salvage

Immediately after the tug sank, Island Tug and Barge went to the site with renowned hard-hat diver Jack Daley. Daley found the wreck and inspected it for the owners and insurance company, although salvagers never worked the wreck. The cost to raise the vessel more than likely exceeded its value as a fifty-eight-year-old wooden tug.

It is rumoured that throughout the 1960s and 70s, sport divers from Vancouver Island visited the site and raised a number of artifacts, including the binnacle, compass, bell, and some portholes. However, this could not be proved and none of the artifacts are known to be in a public institution.

Search and Discovery

On 20 July 1985, a small group of UASBC divers consisting of Gord Esplin, Kevin Robinson, Tom Beasley, and Gord Cawley relocated *Foss* using coordinates supplied by Island Tug and Barge, as well as details of the wreck's depth provided by diver Jack Daley. Tom Beasley shared his observations regarding the wreck in a letter to the Foss Launch and Tug Company.

> Although visibility was only 4-6 feet, it was clear that the wreck is a unique one. There are many brass "collectible" items lying near or in the wreck. The cabins have long since rotted away, but the hull is relatively intact lying on its port side. There is abundant marine life growing on the hull and exposed engine parts.

He also mentioned that the team raised four brass objects to verify the find, and that they are presently being cleaned by UASBC members. Currently, the UASBC only has one *Foss* artifact in its collection (a glass light cover). Two portholes are known to remain in personal collections and have not been accessioned.

A decade later, the UASBC revisited the *Henry Foss* 24 October 1993 and again on 16 April 1994. During those expeditions, divers produced a rough sketch of the site. The depth and poor diving conditions prevented creating a proper scale drawing.

Freehand sketch of the *Henry Foss* by Jacques Marc in October 1993.

Status

The UASBC visited the wreck as part of its re-survey of the Southern Gulf Islands on 18 March 2018. The 1993 team collected the coordinates for the wreck site using Loran "C" (a radio-signal-based system). One of our goals was to find the site and confirm its location using GPS. Jacques Marc approached the Canadian Hydrographic Service, which located what appeared to be the wreck in its multi-beam data. Using this as a starting position, the team then used an onboard forward-looking sonar to pinpoint the wreck. Subsequent dives confirmed its location.

The wreck lies on its port side with the keel exposed along the entire length. Its centreline lies on a heading of 315°, stern to bow. The starboard gunwale lies at 92 feet and the sea floor in the vicinity of the stack is 115 feet, when measured on a 5.6-foot tide.

The wreck has deteriorated significantly since the initial exploration in 1985. Nothing remains of the superstructure, house work or decking. The bow and stern are also heavily impacted by rot and marine borers, such that they are almost unrecognizable. The bow is defined by a large quantity of anchor chain and the anchor winch. The stern is defined by the steering quadrant, rudder and stern bumper made of rubber tires. Large fuel tanks take up much of the hull in the stern portion of the wreck.

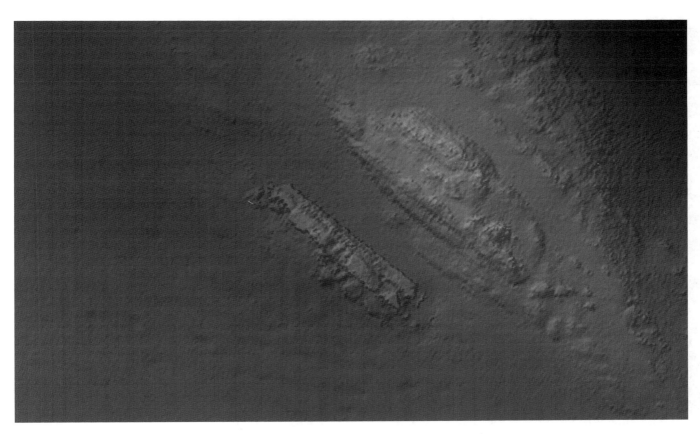

Multi-beam image of *Henry Foss* wreck, courtesy of Parks Canada.

Amidships deep in the hull is the 1,000-hp Enterprise diesel engine. There is also a large concentration of lead acid batteries in the area. The remains of the stack are downslope of the engine and batteries. Forward of the engine is a compressor and high-pressure air tank. The bow contains a water tank and forward of that is the anchor chain locker. The starboard side anchor is on the bottom but still connected to the ship by the anchor chain. The port side hull is buried under mud and debris on the bottom. The starboard hull planking is deteriorating with many holes visible, but is still present roughly to the deck level.

We did not find items like the binnacle, wheel or

portholes, suggesting the reports of salvage by sport divers are true. Divers observed very few small artifacts during the dive. One feature that they did observe was an incandescent light bulb still in its glass waterproof shroud.

At the bequest of the UASBC, Parks Canada's Underwater Archaeology Services Team completed a high-resolution multi-beam survey on the *Henry Foss* on 9 May 2019. The resulting image confirms the diver observations that the *Foss* is falling apart rapidly. The multi-beam image clearly shows that the bow and stern are gone and that the hull is only partially intact on the shallow starboard side.

Conclusions/Recommendations

The *Henry Foss* wreck presents a number of challenges. It is a deep dive, often with current, poor underwater visibility, and on-site hazards like exposed wiring and sharp metal pieces. As such, this dive is not recommended for any but the most experienced divers who have planned adequately.

We must also remember that the loss of the *Foss* was a tragic incident in which several people lost their lives. Although all bodies were recovered, the wreck is a memorial site of sorts. The wreck also still has a number of artifacts that must be protected. While the UASBC has come a long way in terms of educating the diving public in the value of maintaining BC's underwater heritage, we still have a long way to go. The *Heritage Conservation Act* protects all wreck sites, but enforcement is a challenge.

Given our concerns about this site, we believe it is not appropriate to publicize the location of this wreck.

References

Beasley, Thomas F. Correspondence to Foss Launch and Tug Ltd., informing them of the Henry *Foss* find. Letter in UASBC Archives (2 August, 1985).

Griffiths, David W. "Discovery of *Henry Foss*." *Foghorn*, (August 1985), 2-3.

Griffiths, David W. "*Foss* Fuss." *Foghorn*, (September 1986), 4.

Marczyk, John. "*Henry Foss* Survey Dive." *Foghorn*, (July 1994), 12.

Newell, Gordon, ed. *The H. W. McCurdy Marine History of the Pacific Northwest: 1895-1965*, (Seattle: Superior Publishing Co., 1963), 61, 510, 641.

Osborn, Stewart C. *Pacific Motor Boat*, (Seattle: Consolidated Publishing Co., 1946).

Rogers, Fred. *Historic Divers of British Columbia – A History of Hardhat Diving, Salvage and Underwater Construction*, (Duncan: Firgrove Publishing, 2003), 173.

Rogers, Fred. *More Shipwrecks of British Columbia* (Vancouver: Douglas & McIntyre., 1992), 72-73.

Silvestrini, George. "The Historic and Tragic *Henry Foss*." *Foghorn*, Vol. 34, No.1 (2018), 8-9.

Skalley, Michael. Foss*: Ninety Years of Towboating*, (Seattle: Superior Publishing Co., 1981), 141-143.

The San Juan Islander, 5 April 1900.

The Seattle Post Intelligencer, 15 May 1900.

Farrow, Moira. "Divers find wreck of ill-fated tug." *The Vancouver Sun*, 3 August 1985.

Broadfoot, Barry. "6 Perish as Tug Sinks in Gulf Islands Storm." *The Vancouver Sun*, 13 February, 1959.

http://www.tugboatinformation.com/tug.cfm?id=7180

http://saltwaterpeoplehistoricalsociety.blogspot.com/2017/10/henry-foss-1900-1959-cannery-tender-to.html

Steamer *Mary Hare*

Mary Hare at Jubilee Regatta on the Gorge, Victoria. Image F-08842 courtesy of the Royal BC Museum and Archives.

Official Number: 100796

Registry: Canada

Construction

William J. Stephens built the *Mary Hare* in the spring and summer of 1893, launching it in September of that year. A screw-driven steamer, registration documents indicate that the 32-ton vessel measured 73 feet long, 13.6 feet wide, 5.3 feet deep, and had an official number of 100796. Stephens designed it as a wooden-hulled single-decked and masted caravel with a rounded stern. He fitted the *Mary Hare* with two tandem compound surface condensing engines manufactured by Victoria's Albion Iron Works. The cylinders were 9 and 16 inches in diameter, the stroke

was 12 inches, and this generated 11.2 horsepower. The machinery predated the vessel by two years.

Stephens built the *Mary Hare* for Michael Hare, an Irish immigrant who had settled in Victoria as a marine engineer. Michael named the vessel after his daughter, and seems to have intended the steamer to engage in general shipping around the Southern Gulf Islands. After a trial trip on 12 September 1893 from Victoria to Sidney, the vessel would have been a familiar sight around Victoria's harbour.

Operational History

The *Mary Hare* plied the waters around the Southern Gulf Islands, and local advertisements suggest that for the first two years of the vessel's life, it sailed as a freelancer with Hare as captain. The *Daily Colonist* recorded regular visits to New Westminster and Nanaimo, and that the steamer often transported coal, stones, and hay, as well as frequently towing scows and log booms.

In December 1893, the vessel towed a scow laden with lumber to Salt Spring Island. The lumber eventually became a government wharf in Burgoyne Bay, a church in Fulford Harbour, and a handful of new houses in Ganges. On 30 December, Hare accidentally grounded the sealer *Fawn* near Sehl's Point while attempting to tow it out of Victoria for the annual hunt.

In January 1894, Hare towed a hull to Victoria from Port Angeles, and visited Roche Harbour. In March 1894, he towed a log boom from Sidney, and in April Hare transported the effects of Metchosin's well-known quarantine station from Albert Head to William Head, because Albert Head was too exposed to the elements. In May 1894, the *Mary Hare* towed two scows with lumber from Victoria to Saanich and also towed the sealer *Triumph* into Victoria Harbour.

On 24 May 1894, it made trips every twenty minutes to and from the Gorge for the Queen's Birthday Regatta, departing from Broderick's Wharf in the inner harbour. Passengers could pay a quarter for "comfort, speed, safety and to see everything . . . the best accommodation on the route." The following month, it ferried coal from Nanaimo to various ports, and in July it resupplied a work party building a government road near Muir Bay.

A turning point in the *Mary Hare*'s life came in May 1895, when it began servicing the Victoria-Sidney Railroad. *The Daily Colonist* recorded that on the week of 6 May, "the steamer has undergone alterations which entirely change her appearance, and much for the better." Hare had the saloon completely surrounded by windows, removed sleeping quarters because upcoming transits would be short, and installed a promenade deck that sported an awning for summer sailing.

Mary Hare advertisement, *Victoria Daily Colonist*, 3 November, 1895.

The *Colonist* recorded that "the steamer's running schedule . . . will be regulated so that people living in the neighbouring islands can come to town in the morning and return to their homes in the evening." The *Mary Hare*'s new schedule saw her sailing six days a week, leaving either Sidney or Ganges for Mayne, Saturna, Pender, and Moresby islands, Cowichan Wharf, Fulford Harbour, Burgoyne Bay, Vesuvius, and "all other way ports."

Loss

On Thursday, 5 February 1896, the *Mary Hare* struck a rock off Reid Island, where the crew intended to go ashore to collect cordwood. Unable to displace the vessel and resigned to waiting for a change of tide, the crew went ashore to forage for food. The *Colonist* records that, "on their return they saw with dismay that the steamer was in flames and beyond saving. With difficulty one of her boats was secured, and it was in this that her crew afterwards found their way to Chemainus." No theory is proposed for the cause of the fire, although the article does specify that Hare might be able to salvage his vessel "if the machinery can be saved, and it is possible that much of it can," although "the hull is badly burnt. An examination of the remains will be made immediately and at present a man is left in charge."

Salvage

On 11 February 1896, the *Colonist* reported that Captain Hare, a diver, and Captain Collister, Victoria's Inspector of Hulls, travelled to Reid Island on the tug *Constance* for an "official survey" of the wreck. The expedition returned the following day, and reported that "the wrecked vessel at low tide stands high and dry out of the water on the rocks which it struck before the fire occurred. It was found that everything about the craft, other than that which was metal, had been destroyed by the fire; but that the machinery is still good." On 6 March, the *Constance* again sailed for the wreck site intent on salvaging the "machinery of the lost steamer," which T. Magensen purchased from Robert Ward and Company for use in a new vessel.

No further articles could be found that confirm whether the engine and boiler were recovered.

Search and Discovery

During the 1982 Gulf Islands project, the UASBC completed visual swim searches along the western shoreline and around the reefs at the southern extremity of Reid Island. Along the western shore, particularly in the bay, the divers encountered a great deal of human-made debris, such as encrusted and corroded lengths of chain, various engine parts, assorted machinery, as well as the remnants of abandoned wharves and docks.

At the extreme southern end of the bay, slightly west of a series of piles, a set of double railway tracks were discovered extending west into the sea for 87 m. These tracks were apparently used by a fish saltery and boat yard that operated briefly on the island in the 1920s. The marine railway was used to haul barges and vessels needing repairs onto shore. This activity would explain the large amount of debris scattered about in the bay.

Investigations carried out on Reid Island itself found that extensive logging and wood cutting has taken place over the years. There was no clear indication of where the crew of the *Mary Hare* might have been gathering their cordwood fuel. The western shore of Reid Island was chosen as the prime search area as it is a relatively protected temporary anchorage and provides easy access to shore. There

are also three drying rocks very close to the beach, which a vessel could conceivably strike. Underwater searchers paid special attention to this area, although they discovered no debris in the vicinity of the rocks. The divers searching this area used a contour or parallel-to-shore search method that extended up to 100 m from the shore for the entire length of the western shoreline in depths of 5-55 feet.

The second area to be searched was the southern extremity of Reid Island, where there is a large reef system comprising drying, semi-drying, and submerged rock outcrops. We searched this area because the account of the loss clearly states that the *Mary Hare* struck a rock close to shore and stranded upon it before catching fire. The searchers used circular and random searches in this area due to the unevenness of the bottom terrain and the heavy concentration of bull kelp. For six hours, divers thoroughly searched the area in and around the reefs and found no visible trace of wreckage.

The UASBC visited Reid Island twice during the Gulf Islands re-inventory project. Six dives were completed on 10 April 2017 along the eastern shoreline of the island, starting at co-ordinates 49° 00.421' N by 123° 37.789' W and ending at 49° 00.038' N by 123° 37.036' W. We employed contour searches and followed the 20-foot depth contour. During our search we found the bottom along the shoreline to be rock. This transitioned to sand at about 20 feet. The team discovered no evidence of the steamer or debris of any kind.

On 16 March 2019, six additional dives were completed. Divers dropped in at coordinates 49° 00.028' N by 123° 37.046' W and swam to coordinates 48° 59.506' N by 123° 36.884' W. Once again, they used a contour search, but came up empty-handed.

Status

The wreckage of the steamer *Mary Hare* remains undiscovered.

Conclusions/Recommendations

When Hare inspected the wreck on 11 February 1896, he reported that "the wrecked vessel at low tide stands high and dry out of the water on the rocks which it struck before the fire occurred. It was also found that everything about the craft, other than what was metal, had been destroyed by the fire; but that the machinery was still good." If we assume that the engines and boilers were salvaged and that the hull was burnt in its entirety little else would have been left. The fact that the rock dries at low tide also means any bits and pieces could have been picked up by local salvagers at low tide. This may explain

why the UASBC has not been able to find any evidence of the *Mary Hare*.

Just to be certain that there isn't something to be found, the UASBC recommends that further searches be conducted around the north end of the Reid Island with particular attention being given to Rose Islets. If the wreckage is not located in these areas, the UASBC believes that past salvage efforts were so effective that little remains to be found.

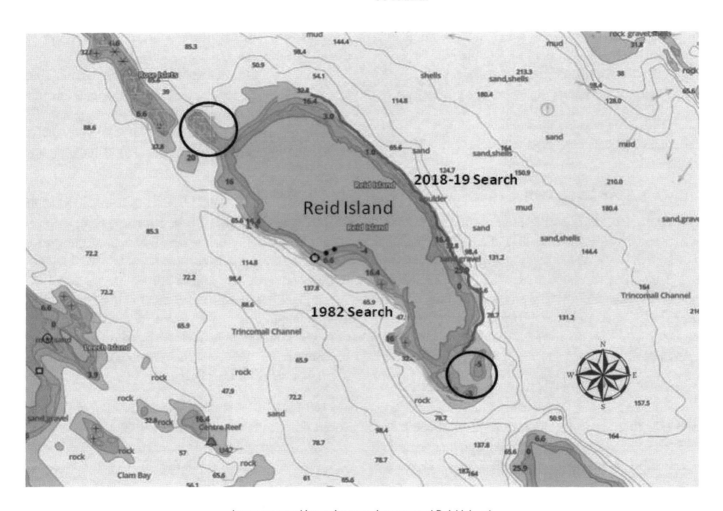

Areas covered by swim searches around Reid Island.

References

BC Archives, Record Group 12, Vol. 373, 38.

BC Archives Record Group 12, Volume 472, Reel C-3184, 91.

BC Archives, GR 123-7, Box 3, File 24.

Mary Hare, Canada Department of Transport, 14/1893.

Mary Hare 100796, Builder's Certificate, Canada Department of Transport, 14/1893.

Mary Hare, Certificate of Survey, 23 August 1893, Canada Department of Transport, 14/1893.

Griffiths, David W. "*Mary Hare.*" *Foghorn*, (1984).

Griffiths, David W. A *Report on the Historic Shipwrecks of the Southern Gulf Islands of British Columbia.* (Vancouver, unpublished, 1982), 39-49.

Andy Lamb, personal communication with J. Marc, 19 February, 2008.

The Daily Colonist, 20 August 1893.

Ibid, 12 September 1893.

Ibid., 7 December 1893.

Ibid., 16 December 1893.

Ibid., 31 December 1893.

Ibid., 20 August 1894.

Ibid, 31 August 1894.

Ibid., 11 January 1894.

Ibid., 30 March 1894.

Ibid., 13 April 1894.

Ibid., 23 May 1894.

Ibid., 10 May 1895.

Ibid., 11 February 1896.

Ibid., 12 February 1896.

Ibid., 13 February 1896.

Ibid, 7 March 1896.

Steamship *Miami*

Miami by Antonio Jacobsen 1897, courtesy of Rehs Galleries, Inc., New York City.

Official Number: 92685

Signal letters: KMPH

Registration: United States

Construction

SS *Miami* began its life as the SS *Nerito*. Sunderland's Short Brothers & Company launched the *Nerito* on 22 September 1891. The English firm had completed construction by 3 November of the same year. They had designed the *Nerito* as a steel freighter. Short Brothers built the vessel for D. G. & T. Pinkney (Pinkney & Sons Steamship Company Ltd.), prominent ship owners of Sunderland. *Nerito* was Hull Number 206.

Its dimensions were 320 feet long, 42 feet wide, and 28 feet deep. *Nerito* measured 2,919 gross tons or 1,872 registered tons. William Allan & Company built the engine, outfitting the vessel with a triple expansion steam engine of 280 nominal hp. The engine cylinders measured 63, 38 ½ and 23½ inches in diameter with a 42-inch stroke. Two cylindrical return tube boilers had 11-foot diameters by 10 feet long with a working pressure of 160 pounds to power the engine. The boilers consumed 17 tons of coal per day, which generated a speed of 8-10 knots. Short Brothers equipped *Nerito* with five steel bulkheads. At launch, Short Brothers rigged *Nerito* as a half brig, suggesting that it fly square sails on the foremast. After an 1894-95 grounding and subsequent repairs, the vessel was recorded as being schooner-rigged. An Antonio Jacobsen painting depicts a clipper style bow.

Operational History

An article published in the *Watertown Daily Times* on 26 August 1892 suggests that D. G. & T. Pinkney experienced financial difficulties shortly after the launch of *Nerito*, and that they placed the management of the company and its vessels in the hands of W. & T. W. Pinkney (Operators of the Columbia Steam Navigation Company and Neptune Steam Navigation Company). *Nerito's* activities are largely unknown between August 1892 and August 1894. Given that the Pinkneys are known to have participated in the coal trade, it is likely that the *Nerito* sailed as a collier.

The *Nerito* left Sunderland at 13:00 on 25 August 1894 with water ballast and 750 tons of bunker coal, bound for Hampton Roads, Virginia, via Halifax (The destination is alternatively given as Baltimore).

On 11 September 1894, *Nerito* ran aground on the eastern bar of Sable Island in dense fog. The crew tried to kedge the ship off the shore, to no avail as the impact had firmly embedded the vessel in the sand bottom. Agreeing that the wreck would shortly break up, the insurance claims were quickly settled, and the vessel was abandoned and even removed from the Lloyd's Register.

The Department of Marine and Fisheries held a formal investigation into the circumstances leading to the stranding and abandonment of the *Nerito* in Halifax between 26-28 September 1894. The Court found that unexpected ocean currents set the vessel northward and eastward of her calculated position and that the Captain William Skipper committed an error of judgment.

The Merritt Wrecking Company of New York applied for and obtained permission to send equipment to the island to float *Nerito*. In October 1894, Merritt put a pump and a boiler aboard the *Nerito* but could do no more due to adverse weather. On 15 June 1895, they returned with wrecking tug *J. D. Jones*. Although it cost $20,000, they successfully raised the *Nerito*. The tug towed it to Halifax and Merritt sold the wreck on 29 June 1895 to stevedores and steamship operators T. Hogan & Sons of New York. The ship's engines were subsequently repaired and the *Nerito* travelled to New York under its own power in late July 1895. The ship's new owners rebuilt the vessel and renamed it *Miami*. They changed the vessel's registration from the United Kingdom to the United States. *Miami* received the new Official Number 92685 and signal letters KMPH.

On 10 July 1897, T. Hogan & Sons formed the Lone Star Line (Miami Steamship Company) using the steamers *Miami, Menemsha,* and *Matteawan* to contest the control that the Mallory and Morgan Lines exerted over the New York to Galveston trade. The 18 July 1897 *New York Times* reported that a bitter battle had erupted between the Mallory Line and the Lone Star Line (T. Hogan & Sons). The battle for shipping supremacy began with a race between the Mallory Steamer *Lampassas* and the Lone Star Line vessel *Miami*, both loaded with cotton, from New York to Galveston. The two ships left New York's harbour on 17 July 1897. On 24 July, it was reported that the *Miami* suffered a fire in its aft compartment and had put in at Key West, Florida. The damage could not have been significant, as *The Record* (American Register of Shipping) does not note any repairs being made until March 1898.

The Morgan Line escalated the squabble on 9 August 1897 by cutting its rate on all freight between New York and Galveston to two cents per hundredweight, down from the usual forty-five to eighty cents. Lone Star responded accordingly and increased the pressure by transporting 272 head of cattle from Galveston to New York at rates below prevailing railroad rates. Although Hogan might have been well intentioned in launching the competition, the strategy proved unsustainable, considering the larger Mallory/Morgan resources. Infuriated, the Lone Star Line took the situation to the federal courts, which ruled in favour of the Mallory Line. In May 1899 Lone Star announced that two of the line's steamers, *Miami* and *Matteawan,* had been sold and that the line would cease operation.

The Pacific Coast Company of San Francisco purchased the *Miami* to carry coal from Puget Sound to San Francisco. The *Miami* arrived in San Francisco from Baltimore on 26 August 1899 to begin its new career. According to the *San Francisco Call*, the *Miami* was making three trips a month carrying coal from BC and Puget Sound ports to San Francisco.

In November 1899 the *Miami's* owners temporarily withdrew

it from the coal trade to carry grain. It arrived at San Francisco from Seattle on 13 November with a load of wheat. When alongside, the vessel collided with the tank steamer *George Loomis* and barkentine *Gleaner*. The *Loomis* lost its after rail and sustained heavy damage to the quarterdeck.

According to the *San Francisco Call* of 1 December 1899, the *Miami* arrived in San Francisco from Seattle, taking six days in heavy weather to make the trip.

Loss

The *Miami* left the coal bunkers at Oyster Harbour (Ladysmith, BC) early on the morning of 25 January 1900, in the charge of Pilot Butler. The *Miami* struck White Rock during high tide. Upon impact, the reef ripped an immense gash in the vessel's hull. The bulkheads initially kept the water out, but as the tide dropped and the vessel settled, they gave way. Shortly after the grounding, the first officer and three crewmen left in one of the boats to notify the owners and to summon assistance.

The tugs *Lorne* and *Pilot* and the collier *Bristol* were sent from Victoria to help. However, at 17:00 the *Miami* began to separate just under the bridge, and the two halves parted. When the tugs arrived, they did not even make an attempt to save the vessel as the collier had filled with water and had already partially sunk.

The British Colonist reported that on the morning of 26 January there was a gaping hole in the hull from the waterline up, extending through the ship. The paper further reported that the bow had settled down on one side of the reef and the stern on the other. The paper confirmed that the fracture had occurred beneath the bridge and that very little of the ship was above water at high tide.

The *Miami* had 4,500 tons of coal on board, and was worth about $150,000 with a number of parties holding insurance. Insurers held $19,000 in San Francisco offices, while others held $2,500 in Victoria, with the remainder in England. The recipients of the cargo had not insured their coal.

Captain Gibson, a United States Consular agent, and also an agent for the insurance company at Chemainus, took charge of the wreck and engaged the tug *Pilot* to stand by and assist in saving the gear.

In response to allegations that authorities had not accurately charted the reef, the officers of the HMS *Egeria* re-surveyed the reef on 31 January 1900. They concluded that the rock which the *Miami* struck had been previously charted with perfect accuracy.

Salvage

Miami, along with its engines, boilers, tackle apparel, and furniture, was sold by public auction on 13 February 1900. Cahn & Cohen of Seattle paid $4,000 for the wreck and announced that they planned to break up it up and remove all valuable materials. Work would begin four to six weeks after the auction.

Fortuitously, the tug *Sadie* arrived in Victoria from Puget Sound on 24 March, towing the big scow *Ajax*, which Cahn & Cohen would use to salvage the wreck. Victoria-based deep sea diver J. McHardie prepared the scow for its task. Cahn & Cohen successfully saved the boilers, chains, and other items from *Miami*. Between the tug *Vancouver* and scow *Ajax*, all the equipment landed in Seattle on 20 May 1900. Interestingly, The American Tug Boat Company used *Miami*'s steering wheel in the vessel *Augusta*, which was scrapped in 1940.

It is not clear how much of the coal Cahn & Cohen salvaged from the wreck. Also, the ship *Louis Walsh*, which supported salvage operations, had a narrow escape from total destruction. While the *Walsh*'s crew salvaged the *Miami*'s remains, the *Walsh* broke free and drifted onto the reef. Other vessels pulled it off the reef the next day with the loss of its anchor and 75 feet of chain. The tug *Pilot* towed the *Walsh* to sea en route to San Francisco on 20 February.

In November 1900, in response to the *Miami* wreck, the CGS *Quadra* placed a large red buoy on the north end of the reef extending from White Rock in Stuart Channel.

In 1956, John Peters salvaged the vessel's propeller shafting and other metals. Fred Rogers explored the wreck in 1960, but reported that he found very little of interest. Gary Bridges, a Vancouver diver, found a port hole on the wreck as late as 1978.

Remains of *Miami* as seen at low tide in the 1970s, courtesy of UASBC Archives.

Status

The UASBC first investigated the *Miami* as part of its Gulf Islands survey in 1980-82. However, there is no record in UASBC files of what work was accomplished.

After a long hiatus, the UASBC re-visited the site on 21 March 2009. On this trip, divers placed floats on either end of the wreck and they collected GPS coordinates at the bow and stern for possible future work. In August 2011, the UASBC placed an interpretive plaque aboard the *Miami* to commemorate its sinking.

The UASBC dived the *Miami* wreck twice as part of the Gulf Islands re-inventory project: once on 9 April 2017 and again on 24 February 2019, completing twelve on-site person-dives.

A physical datum off-set survey was not completed, as the wreck was considered to be too badly broken up with too few ship fittings remaining. However, a tape measure was run down the centreline of the wreck to get an overall site length measurement, and to serve as a reference for making on-site observations. The sternpost of the wreck was found in 8 m of water on a 2.1-m tide at coordinates 49° 02.381' N by 123° 42.792' W. The bow is an unrecognizable jumble, but the wreckage that defines the bow area is at 49° 02.399' N by 123° 42.729' W. The wreck lies on a 076° heading stern to bow, and the distance from the sternpost to the end of the bow wreckage is 85 m. Three tail shaft bushing assemblies define the centreline of the ship as one swims forward from the sternpost. The first shaft bushing is 22 m from the sternpost, the second is at 27.56 m and the third is at 33.15 m.

The third shaft bushing was found to be in 4.2 m of water. The shaft bushings are 40 cm long by 27 cm wide. Since width equals diameter, the propeller shaft would have been 27 cm (10.6 inches) in diameter. At the third bushing, the hull was 12.85 m (42 feet) wide, equalling the *Miami's* original width. The UASBC interpretive plaque is 4 m to the port side of the third bushing. Forward of the third bushing, the wreck becomes a jumble of collapsed steel plates, knees, and beams. The portion of the hull that remains is essentially the lower flooring to the turn of the bilge on either side.

Extant hull to turn of bilge on *Miami* wreck.
Photo courtesy of Ewan Anderson.

The shallowest point on the wreck occurs at roughly amidships and was 8 feet (2.4 m) on a 6.9-foot tide. In the stern and near the bow, there was planking visible on the bottom. This was most likely wooden ceiling material that lined the holds.

Overall, the hull is quite scenic, being covered with plumose anemones and seasonal bull kelp. There is still a considerable amount of coal on site, especially at either end of the vessel. Aside from the three shaft bushings, divers found no other pieces of the ship's machinery and no small artifacts on the site.

Conclusions and Recommendations

The best time to dive the *Miami* is in winter, when the plankton levels are low and underwater visibility can exceed 6-7 m. In spring and summer, the plankton bloom can reduce underwater visibility to 1 m or less. The fact that this wreck is extremely shallow, experiences poor underwater visibility, and has few artifacts of interest means it is seldom visited. There is already an underwater interpretive plaque on the wreck.

The UASBC has no recommendations for this site. The existing *Heritage Conservation Act* protection should be sufficient to protect what is left of this wreck.

References

American Lloyd's Register of American & Foreign Shipping, 1892-1900.

http://library.mysticseaport.org/initiative/SPSearch.cfm?ID=617002

Blume, Kenneth J. *Historical Dictionary of the US Maritime Industry*, (Maryland: The Scarecrow Press Inc., 2012), 224.

Francaviglia, Richard V. *From Sail to Steam: Four Centuries of Texas Maritime History, 1500-1900*, (Austin: University of Texas Press, 1998).

Griffiths, David W. *A Report on the Historic Shipwrecks of the Southern Gulf Islands of British Columbia.* (Vancouver, unpublished, 1982), 131-135.

Newell, Gordon, ed. *The H. W. McCurdy Marine History of the Pacific Northwest: 1895-1965*, (Seattle: Superior Publishing Co., 1963), 50, 63, 484.

Rogers, Fred. *Shipwrecks of British Columbia* (Vancouver, 1976), 53-55.

San Francisco Call, 27 August 1899.

Ibid., 14 November 1899.

Ibid., 1 December 1899.

Ibid., 27 January 1900.

Ibid., 1 February 1900.

Ibid., 14 February 1900.

"Twenty-Sixth Annual Report of the Department of Marine and Fisheries," (Printed by S. E. Dawson, Printer to the Queen's Most Excellent Majesty, 1894), 24.

The Daily Colonist, 26 January 1900.

Ibid., 27 January 1900.

Ibid., 28 January 1900.

Ibid., 1 February 1900.

Ibid., 2 February 1900.

Ibid., 4 February 1900.

Ibid., 6 February 1900.

Ibid., 7 February 1900.

Ibid., 14 February 1900.

Ibid., 15 February 1900.

Ibid., 20 February 1900.

Ibid., 22 February 1900.

Ibid., 21 March 1900.

Ibid., 6 April 1900.

Ibid., 20 May 1900.

Ibid., 16 June 1900.

Ibid., 4 November 1900.

Urquhart, Colin, ed. *The American Stationer*, Vol XLII (New York: Howard Lockwood & Co., 12 August, 1897), 261.

https://books.google.ca/books?id=qF9YAAAAYAAJ&pg=PA261

http://www.shipscribe.com/usnaux/AW/aw-iris.html

http://www.searlecanada.org/sunderland/sunderland079.html#nerito

http://www.teesbuiltships.co.uk/index.php

https://issuu.com/anmmuseum/docs/flags_national_and_mercantile_for_t

https://novascotia.ca/museum/wrecks/wrecks/shipwrecks.asp?ID=3567

Clipper Ship *Panther*

An American clipper ship similar in size and rig to *Panther*. Painting by Eugene Grandin. (Source undocumented).

Official Number: None

Registry: United States

Construction

Paul Curtis of East Boston built and launched the Clipper ship *Panther* in 1854. Several sources describe the vessel as being a medium clipper. Medium clippers had a sharp bow to cut through the water and flat floors, designed for both speed and carrying cargo. The *Alta California* described the *Panther* as "one the best built ships ever entering the Port of San Francisco." Curtis built *Panther* of oak and fastened it with copper and iron. Further, he diagonally braced the ship with iron straps in the lower hold and between decks. Curtis employed solid wood up to the bilge, and he over-bolted every knee in the ship.

In some cases, he used no fewer than thirty-two bolts in each knee. The overall dimensions were 193.7 feet long, 37.5 feet wide, and 24 feet deep. At the time of its launch, *Panther* was recorded as 1,260 tons. Curtis designed it as a two-decked vessel with three square-rigged masts. He built *Panther* for R. C. Mackay & Sons of Boston, the vessel's registered home port for much of its career.

Operational History

Panther sailed out of Boston on its maiden voyage under the command of Captain Nat G. Weeks for its new owners on 4 March 1854. This transit would become the first of three voyages to Calcutta (present-day Kolkata) carrying railroad iron from England to help build the East Indian Railway. R. C. Mackay dispatched his son, George H. Mackay, as supercargo on the *Panther* to oversee the operations in India.

On the first voyage, it took Weeks only ninety-nine days to reach Calcutta. The *Panther* made the return voyage to Liverpool in one hundred days. The vessel bettered its time on the second voyage, arriving in Calcutta in ninety-three days. *Panther*'s third voyage established it as a capable ship able to handle rough weather: on leaving Calcutta it encountered a series of ferocious storms and nearly foundered, having sprung a leak that forced it to return to port. However, Curtis constructed *Panther* admirably, and once repaired, the vessel made its best run yet, leaving Calcutta's Sand Heads on 16 January 1857 and arriving in Boston on 17 April 1857, ninety-one days later.

On 10 December 1857, Mackay sold *Panther* to Minot & Hooper of Boston, who gave Captain J. P. Gannett command of the ship. The owners then consigned or chartered *Panther* to the Glidden & Williams Line of California Packets. *Panther* transited from Boston to San Francisco on its first voyage under new owners. A bill of lading from that voyage specified that it carried cargo shipped by the Boston Sugar Refinery to San Francisco.

Panther cleared Boston 9 July 1857 and arrived at San Francisco on 30 November after a transit of 143 days. The *San Francisco Shipping Intelligence* recorded it with merchandise to Flint, Peabody & Company. The details of the passage are: thirty-one days to the equator on the Atlantic, sixty-nine days to Cape Horn, 118 days to the equator and San Francisco on the Pacific side.

The *Panther*'s next voyaged to Valparaiso, Chile, on 6 January 1858. The cargo was of a wide assortment of merchandise valued at $16,892.97, including:

- 50 barrels smoked salmon
- 250 boxes candles
- 86 rolls matting
- 313 pkgs firecrackers
- 12 cases merchandise
- 200 pkgs mess beef
- 3 d (*sic*) sugar
- 73 kegs tallow

- 1,990 bags California beans

The *Panther* made a quick (thirty-eight-day) trip from San Francisco to Valparaiso, arriving on 12 April 1858. Gannett made the return trip from Valparaiso to San Francisco in fifty days, arriving in early June. The cargo consisted of 1,800 barrels of Chilean flour, 450 tons of Chilean coal and 182 packages of Chilean peaches.

After a brief port visit, *Panther* departed San Francisco for Calcutta on 5 July 1858, carrying unspecified cargo. It departed Sandheads of Calcutta on 28 March 1859 and was ninety-nine days en route back to New York. At some point, *Panther* returned to San Francisco, as it is next reported departing that city on 27 February 1860 for Callao, Peru, to load guano. From Callao it returned to New York via Hampton Roads. The voyage took ninety-two days. Next, the vessel crossed to Liverpool and then on to Calcutta and Bombay, arriving back in Boston on 31 August 1862.

In fall 1862, Minot & Hopper reportedly sold *Panther* to Randolph M. Cooley & Company. The vessel subsequently became part of the Merchant Express Line of Clipper Ships. This fact is confusing as *American Lloyd's Register of American & Foreign Shipping* continues to record it as being owned by Minot & Hooper. It is more likely that Merchant Express Line became the managing operators or shipping agents for the ship, while ownership probably remained with Minot & Hooper.

Clipper ship advertising card, circa 1863-1866.

Nevertheless, a clipper ship advertising card from around 1862-1866 lists *Panther* as being dispatched from New York to San Francisco by the Merchants Express Line and identifies Sylvester Lothrop as captain. *Panther* cleared New York on 22 December 1862, and Lothrop completed his first voyage between the two ports in 140 days, arriving at San Francisco on 10 May 1863 with a cargo consigned to DeWitt, Kittle & Company. The *Panther* next sailed for Callao, making a swift run of forty-five days, arriving on 27 July 1863. In September 1865 *Panther* sailed for Baker's Island, in the south-central Pacific for a load of Guano, which citizens of the day considered to be the next "gold rush."

Clipper Ship Advertising Card C. 1868 advertising August 27, 1868 Panther New York to San Francisco Voyage.

The list of cargo aboard *Panther* on its 7 January 1868 trip to New York.

In September 1867, *Panther* was sold to Pope & Talbot of San Francisco for $25,000. The Talbots planned to use it not only for carrying lumber from Port Gamble to ports like San Francisco and New York, but also to carry general merchandise in the rising trade with Hong Kong and Canton (China). As a result of *Panther*'s sale, Captain Lothrop was replaced by Captain Fred Johnson, who made a single round-trip voyage on the vessel. *Panther* cleared San Francisco 7 January 1868, bound for New York with cargo consigned by Moore & Company. The crew struggled to round the horn, having to dodge large icebergs en route.

On 27 July 1868 *Panther* departed New York for San Francisco carrying 250 tons of rails for the San Jose Road consigned to J. H. Coghill & Company.

In early 1869, Pope & Talbot hired Captain A. K. Kilton to captain *Panther*. Under Kilton's command *Panther* sailed along the Australian coastline from Newcastle, New South Wales, to Melbourne and then Sydney in 1869. In 1870 it transited between San Francisco and Hong Kong in speedy round trips, taking only forty-four days each way. In the early 1870s, it plied the waters between San Francisco, Vancouver, and Honolulu.

By late 1872, *Panther* had entered in the coastal trade, regularly shipping coal from Nanaimo to San Francisco and returning in ballast to stop and pick up lumber and materials from mills in Port Townsend. At some point in early in 1873, John W. Balch became captain. Entry clearance records show that he made monthly trips between San Francisco and Nanaimo, with an average transit time in each direction of eight days.

On the morning of 15 January 1874, the coastal steamer *Emma* arrived in Victoria from Nanaimo and reported that *Panther*'s crew had loaded coal and would slip shortly.

Loss

The *Panther* cleared Nanaimo loaded with 1,750 tons of coal on the evening of Saturday, 17 January 1874, bound for San Francisco. The steam tug *Goliah* took the *Panther* under tow and the crew had instructions to transit to the open waters of the Strait of Juan de Fuca. A strong southeast wind blew as the vessels departed Nanaimo with snow blowing and seas beginning to swell.

Statements provided to the *British Colonist* by Captain Balch of *Panther* and Captain Libby of the tug *Goliah* convey what happened the night of *Panther's* loss.

Captain Libby reported that by 20:30, the two vessels had reached Turn Point, with the wind gusting strongly and the tide ebbing. Libby reported that he signalled to the crew of the *Panther* to get her fore and aft canvas set, but says that the clipper's crew did not comply. By this time, *Panther* had become unmanageable. The ship had hoisted no sail, and *Goliah* drifted steadily toward Pender Island. By 23:15 the *Panther's* weight dragged the steamer astern so swiftly that the engine could not pass centres. Captain Libby decided that he had to cut the towing hawser to save the tug, and issued orders to that effect. A few minutes later *Panther* flashed a bright light, then struck broadside on a rock. The sea made a clean sweep over it from stem to stern. Captain Libby reported his inability to render assistance as a result of the mountainous seas. Every moveable object onboard the *Goliah* had been washed overboard, and the windows in the forward house had been staved in. *Goliah's* crew put their all towards saving the tug.

According to Libby, he could still see the *Panther's* lights at 03:00, and by 04:00 the wind gradually moderated and the seas begin to subside. The *Goliah* cruised past the site of the wreck at daylight but could not find any evidence of the ship or its crew. The *Goliah* continued to search for *Panther* for twenty-four hours. Libby finally abandoned the search on Monday and headed for Seattle, where he reported the loss of *Panther* and the crew. Unknown to Libby, the *Panther's* crew had survived the wreck.

Meanwhile, the testimony of Captain Balch makes clear that immediately after Libby had the hawser cut, he set his canvas and tried to beat (tack) offshore. However, at about 02:00 *Panther* struck a rock, lifted about six feet out of the water and bounded over it. Seriously damaged and taking on water, Captain Balch decided to run for Trincomali Channel and beach the vessel.

Shortly before daylight, the wind carried *Panther* stern first onto a reef that juts out from the south end of Wallace Island. This time Balch couldn't escape. *Panther*

settled to the bottom, leaving only its rigging and port side rail above the water. Balch, his wife, the officers, and the crew made it safely off the *Panther* to Beggs Settlement (present-day Fernwood) on Salt Spring Island across from the wreck. Here, Mr. Sampson and other settlers attended to their needs.

The steamer *Emma* brought news of the *Panther's* loss and the probable loss of the *Goliah* upon returning from Nanaimo on Thursday, 22 January. Fortunately, the steamer *North Pacific* arrived soon after from Puget Sound with news that the *Goliah* had arrived safely in Seattle. The *Emma's* crew reported that when they saw the *Panther* on Wednesday, it was submerged to the weather rail. The *Emma* carried dispatches that Balch had written to his superiors.

Upon hearing the news, the *North Pacific* sailed on the evening of 22 January for the scene of the wreck to assist in saving the gear and furniture.

Salvage

The steamer *Prince Alfred* provided an update on the situation at the wreck on 1 February 1874. The crew reported that *Panther* lay on its beam-ends (on its side) on a reef about 1,260 fathoms from a point on Narrow Island, in 6 fathoms at low water. The sails and running gear had been sent ashore, except the braces. The *Alfred's* crew thought that it would be possible to save all the spars and standing rigging, except the lower rigging, which they could not access, the lee rail being underwater at low tide. Captain Balch considered the cargo of coal a total loss, as the ship remained submerged at low tide (except the weather-rail). The captain and crew intended to remain camped on the shore near the wreck until they received orders from the owners and underwriters.

On 11 March 1874, the *Alfred* delivered powerful pumps to the wreck site for a second attempt to raise the wrecked ship. By 25 March 1874, all attempts to raise *Panther* had failed. The salvage crews and ship's company abandoned the wreck. Messrs. Myers & Franks bought the wreck and cargo for $1,500 on Monday, 20 April 1874, when the owners auctioned it off on San Francisco's

Merchants Exchange.

Captain Gilbert, the agent for Messrs. Myers & Franks, arrived in Victoria during the week of 4 May to charter a schooner in an attempt to raise the vessel. He planned to first remove the remaining standing rigging, send down divers to remove the coal (1,755 tons), and then place camels under the hull to raise the vessel. Gilbert visited the wreck on 7 May and found the deck about 10 feet out of water at low tide.

On 12 October 1874, Gilbert gave public notice that he had sold his entire interest in the wreck to James Waterman of Portland, and would not be held responsible for any debts contracted on behalf of the wreck.

Search and Discovery

The wreck's location was known well before divers began exploring it in the late 1950s and early 1960s. Stories abound that when the vessel was more intact, the locals would go out to it on extreme low tides and collect coal for use in their stoves and fireplaces.

Status

The first official record of diving on the wreck appears in the 6 June 1963 edition of the *Gulf Islands Driftwood*. It reported that the Fathom Phantom Divers (a Salt Spring Island dive club) located and dived on the wreck in 40 feet of water off Panther Point.

Fred Rogers reports in his book *Shipwrecks of British Columbia* that he visited the wreck in 1964 and hoisted a large section of timbers out of the water. He states that the vessel had been well built, being held together with large brass rods, spikes of various sizes, and the occasional hardwood dowel and wedge. Before returning the timbers to the wreck, he removed several brass rods.

In 1975, a permit for an archaeological workshop on the *Panther* was issued to Henry Rosenthal of the Centre for Continuing Education at the University of BC. The permit application stated that the intent of the workshop was to instruct up to fifteen students in the techniques of exploration, survey, excavation, and conservation. The workshop occurred over 16-22 June 1975. Unfortunately, the students did not produce a report on the workshop.

In April 1979, the Heritage Branch received a one-page report stating that participants employed underwater still photography, sketches, airlifting and jetting to explore and survey the site. The report also indicated that the students raised a small block of wood and two spikes to demonstrate conservation procedures. The fate of the artifacts remains unknown.

The workshop participants were so elated with their experience that a subset of the class formed the UASBC on 20 August 1975, and used an image of what was thought to be the *Panther* as the society logo. It turns out that the image used is that of a sister ship the *Reaper*, which was converted from a ship to a barque.

The UASBC visited the *Panther* as part of completing its status report on the historic shipwrecks of the Gulf Islands in 1980-82. However, the report does not mention what the team accomplished.

Between 22-26 September 2016, the UASBC spent fifty dives exploring and mapping *Panther*. It is located off the southern end of Wallace Island. The stern is 150 m south of Panther Point and 90 m north of the navigation marker on Panther Rock, on the west side of the reef. The coordinates are latitude 48° 55.833' N by longitude 123° 32.032' W.

The wreck lies on a sand-shell bottom parallel to the reef on a 130° heading, stern to bow, with its port side resting up against the reef and the starboard side lying in deeper water. The depth at the stern was 32 feet on a 9.4-foot tide. All that remains of the *Panther*'s once proud clipper ship hull is a shallow cradle-like portion that extends two-thirds of the vessel's length, filled with pieces of encrusted coal. In effect, it is the portion of hull that would have extended from the keel to the turn of the bilge, with the bow and stern missing. Only when one swims over the row of extant frames and copper sheathing on the starboard side does it become apparent that one is on a wreck. The upper deck cabins, main deck, and most of the hull have long since disintegrated due to wave action and marine borers.

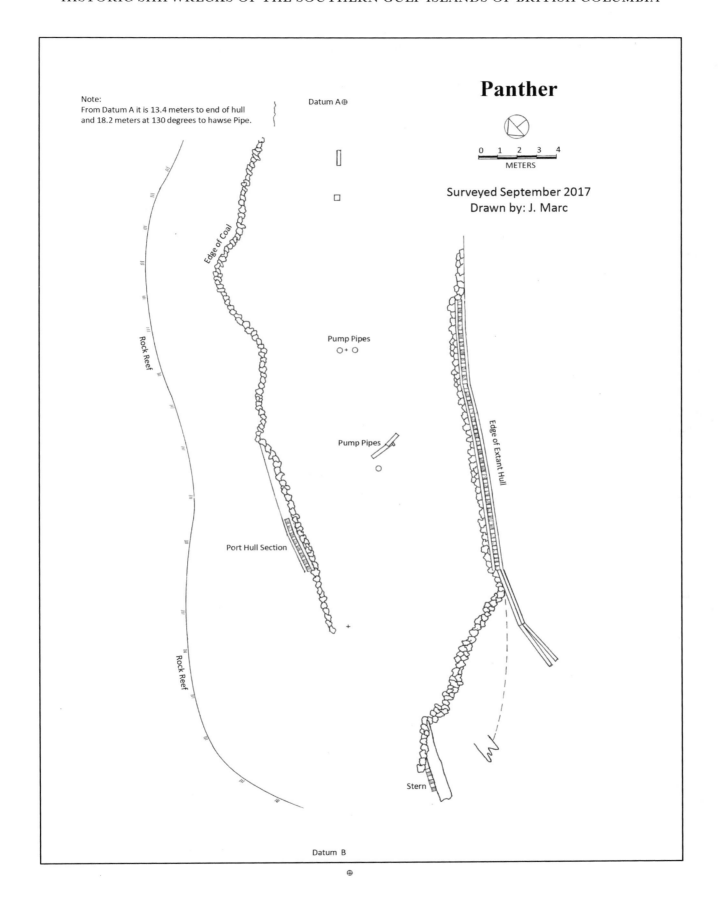

Panther

Surveyed September 2017
Drawn by: J. Marc

Note:
From Datum A it is 13.4 meters to end of hull
and 18.2 meters at 130 degrees to hawse Pipe.

Datum A ⊕

0 1 2 3 4
METERS

Edge of Coal

Rock Reef

Pump Pipes

Pump Pipes

Port Hull Section

Rock Reef

Edge of Extant Hull

Stern

Datum B
⊕

Divers used a datum offset survey to document the wreck. They started by establishing a 41-metre baseline down the centreline of the wreckage. Datum A was established near the bow and datum B marks the stern of the wreckage. Starting at the stern, the only thing visible is some extant stern hull planking protruding out from under the coal cargo. As one moves forward along the centreline of the wreck, a short section (6 m) of the extant port hull becomes visible on the left side of the baseline, at the 16-m mark.

Continuing forward all that can be seen is coal until the first set of pump pipes are reached 21.5 m up the baseline. A second set of pump pipes are visible 28 m up the baseline. These are very diagnostic artifacts. They would extend from the main deck down to the bilge. Leakage pooled amidships so the pump was usually just behind the main mast. In the case of the *Panther*, the UASBC found two sets of pump pipes, suggesting there were two pumping stations. The positions of the pump pipes suggest that one set was just aft of the foremast and the second set were near the mizzen mast.

The extant hull on the starboard side becomes visible 16 m up and 7 m to the right of the baseline. The starboard hull rises 1-2 m from the seafloor and continues uninterrupted for 15 m, terminating about 31 m up the baseline. This section of hull is very diagnostic. The inner ceiling planking, frames, outer hull planking, and copper sheathing are all intact and clearly visible. The average frame size is 20 by 25 cm. Forward of datum A the bow section has completely disintegrated. It is separated from the rest of the hull by 20 m and is identified by two steel hawse pipes and some anchor chain. David Griffiths mentions a capstan near the bow in the original 1982 report, but this could not be found again.

Conclusions/Recommendations

The *Panther* is intrinsically linked to the history of the UASBC. The society was formed as the direct result of a University of British Columbia continuing education course that used the wreck for an underwater archaeology course.

The *Panther* has not been a popular wreck dive in recent years as there are few significant artifacts on site and there is little marine life growing on it (it is not a pretty wreck). During the 1980s it was used by a few charter boat operators for wreck diving courses as it is a shallow, protected and relatively safe to dive. Today there are very few dive charter boats operating in the Gulf Islands, and most are interested in the artificial reef sites.

The UASBC placed an educational plaque on the *Panther* in November 1983. Divers observed during the survey dives that the plaque is deteriorating and should be replaced in the next two years. The 1982 report recommended that a thorough excavation should be completed on the wreck to survey it and to recover any remaining artifacts.

Today, excavation work is not in the UASBC mandate unless there is a compelling case to do so.

The original report also recommended that a concerted effort be made to locate all the artifacts raised from the *Panther*, so that they can be photographed and documented for posterity. This is something that should be done soon, as many of the early divers are now in their 70s or 80s, and both the artifacts and information will be lost when they pass.

References

American Lloyd's Register of American & Foreign Shipping, 1859-1874.
Daily Alta California, 1 December 1857.
Ibid., 10 December 1857.
Ibid., 11 December 1857.
Ibid., 7 January 1858.
Ibid., 26 January 1858.
Ibid., 30 May 1858.
Ibid., 27 February 1860.
Ibid., 11 May 1863.
Ibid., 6 June 1863.
Ibid., 2 May 1865.
Ibid., 20 May 1865.
Ibid., 30 November 1867.
Ibid., 8 January 1868.
Ibid., 27 July 1868.
Ibid., 12 January 1869.

Ibid., 14 January 1869.

Ibid., 11 January 1870.

Ibid., 8 August 1870.

Ibid., 14 September 1870.

Ibid., 14 October 1870.

Ibid., 9 February 1871.

Ibid., 1 September 1871.

Ibid., 16 September 1871.

Ibid., 18 December 1872.

Ibid., 23 December 1872.

Ibid., 27 December 1872.

Ibid., 20 September 1873.

Ibid., 21 November 1873.

Ibid., 22 November 1873.

Daily British Colonist, 12 May 1865.

Ibid., 28 August 1873.

Ibid., 11 September 1873.

Ibid., 30 October 1873.

Ibid., 23 January 1874.

Ibid., 1 March 1874.

Ibid., 7 March 1874.

Ibid., 11 March 1874.

Ibid., 25 March 1874.

Ibid., 28 March 1874.

Ibid., 9 May 1874.

Evening Journal, Adelaide, 26 August, 1869.

Geelong Advertiser, 27 August 1869.

Knoblock, Glenn A. *The American Clipper Ship, 1845–1920: A Comprehensive History, with a Listing of Builders and Their Ships,* (Jefferson: McFarland &Co., 2014).

Mathews, Frederick C. *American Merchant Shops 1850-1900, Series 1*, (New York: Dover Publications, 1987)., 179.

Owens and Murray, Sydney, 27 August, 1869.

The Wallaroo Times & Mining Journal, 4 September 1869.

The Herald Melbourne, 31 August 1869.

Wright, E. W., ed. *Lewis & Dryden's Marine History of the Pacific Northwest*, (New York: Antiquarian Press, Ltd., 1961), 221.

http://bbprivateer.ca/panther

http://www.bruzelius.info/Nautica/Shipbuilding/Shipyards/Clippers(MA).html

https://www.worthpoint.com/worthopedia/1857-clipper-ship-panther-bill-lading-1412337861

http://library.mysticseaport.org/initiative/SPSearch.cfm?ID=617002

Steam Tug *Point Grey*

Steam Tug *Point Grey* as it looked in 1945, courtesy of Vancouver Maritime Museum Collection LM2017.999.007.

Official Number: 130917

Registry: Canada

Construction

Wallace Shipyards constructed and launched the steam tug *Point Grey* at their North Vancouver yard in 1912, under contract to the federal government's Ministry of Public Works. The vessel initially displaced 300 gross tons and was 93.4 feet long, 22.3 feet wide, and 14.5 feet deep. It was equipped with a 62 nominal hp Campbell and Calderwood compound steam engine, built in Paisley, Scotland, and was the only steel tug launched by Wallace Shipyards. Machinists McDougall & Jenkins Company of North Vancouver installed the engine, and the *Point Grey* was issued Official Number 130917. At the same time, the Ministry of Public Works also ordered the *Point*

Ellice, a wood tug similar in specifications to its sister ship, the *Point Grey*.

Operational History

Little is known about *Point Grey*'s service to the Ministry of Public Works. Its first sea trial took place in November 1911 around Vancouver Harbour, and it later operated on the Fraser River towing dredging scows. On 9 December 1913, it collided with an unknown vessel in Burrard Inlet.

The outbreak of the First World War created strong demand for high-grade Sitka spruce and other premium lumber found throughout British Columbia. Military procurement experts identified such lumber as critical for the construction of aircraft.

As such the Imperial Munitions Board (IMB), through its Department of Aeronautical Supplies, "undertook to obtain unlimited amounts of spruce for use in aircraft construction. The IMB also required a lesser, but still a substantial amount, of select quality fir found in the mainland coastal inlets and adjoining islands for the same purpose."

To transport the logs from logging camps to the saw mills, the IMB also needed tugs. The Department of Public Works loaned both the *Point Grey* and *Point Ellice* to the IMB; however, both tugs needed to be lengthened "in order to be suitable for towing Davis rafts across Hecate Strait's shallow waters, which during storms, develops a violent wave action."

The IMB sent the *Point Grey* back to Wallace Shipyards, where workers expanded the tug to 105 feet long, 44.2 feet wide, and 27.8 feet deep. The retrofit also increased the tonnage by 62 tons to a total of 300 tons. Despite the laudable wartime conversion, Wallace didn't complete the work until September 1918, shortly before the conclusion of hostilities. Nevertheless, *Point Grey* did tow rafts in the war's aftermath, including rafts that contained lumber initially ordered by the IMB. On 17 November 1920, the Ministry of Public works advertised the tug as available to rent. During the later years of the stalwart tug's service, BC Steamship Service chartered it for towing rail barges between Vancouver and Victoria.

Point Grey aground on Virago Rock, courtesy of Vancouver maritime Museum Collection LM2017-999-011.

Loss

Point Grey ran aground on Virago Rock in Porlier Pass while navigating dense fog on the evening of 26 February 1949. Captain John C. Hill took a barge of railway cars under tow in Vancouver, and entered the pass at 11:00 after navigating the dense fog bank engulfing the Strait of Georgia and surrounding Gulf Islands. Unfortunately for Hill, after initially hitting Virago Rock, the rail barge in tow maintained its forward momentum, colliding with the stricken tug and further impaling it on the rock. The two men manning the barge cut the hawser connecting it to the tug and anchored safely, while *Point Grey*'s radio operator transmitted a distress call after the grounding. The tug gradually began to list as the tide fell, prompting Hill and the eleven-man crew to lower a lifeboat and flee the wreck.

Salvage

A Straits Towing and Salvage rescue vessel came to the aid of the shipwrecked men, and the company's tug, *Salvor*, arrived shortly thereafter. Next, the tug *Malaspina Straits*, along with two scows, took station on the wreck, but a thick oil sheen made salvage work difficult. The salvage crew consisted of fifteen men under George Unwin. Additionally, the *Vancouver Daily Province* reported that the

> rise and fall of sea levels is so narrow that salvage workers have been hampered in their efforts to seal portions of the ship which might be pumped dry to help float her free. Meanwhile, as the days pass, the vessel's costly engines and other equipment inside the hull suffer more and more from the deadly effect of salt water on fine metal.

A week after the grounding, the salvagers eventually succeeded in welding shut all of *Point Grey*'s portholes and hatches, and had pumped out the wreck to the best of their ability, but the stricken tug would not budge. The unsuccessful attempt to raise the wreck caused salvagers to question whether the hull should be considered a "total constructive loss" meaning "that salvage and repairs would cost more than the tug is worth."

At some point in mid-April, Island Tug and Barge divers Jack Collins and Jack Pitt made a discovery that would negate the possibility of raising the tug. The divers had a theory that the hull had been severely penetrated by rock. The *Vancouver Daily Province* reported that Collins made

> a dangerous entry down into the oil and water filled hull through a deck opening. He had to pass through 10 inches of heavy fuel oil floating on the water surface inside, then grope his way down into the engine room while his diving partner clung to the entrance outside ready to rescue him if something went wrong . . . but the diver found what he feared he would, an ugly rock holding the half submerged *Point Grey* like a great spike.

They reported that the rock "ripped through the steel hull like paper, tore a hole 10 feet by 16 feet and came to a stop alongside the boiler."

Around a month after the salvage conducted by Straits Towing, a second outfit, Island Tug and Barge, arrived at the wreck site to continue the work (after the dive made by Collins and Pitt). Island Tug and Barge succeeded in removing much of *Point Grey*'s deck gear before abandoning the wrecked tug, which "lies half out of the water on her right side, her bow pointing grotesquely skyward…a grim reminder of the dangers which lurk beneath the surface in this and other narrow British Columbia passes through which vessels must navigate day in and day out."

Search and Discovery

The *Point Grey* was visible on Virago Rock for fourteen years before sinking, so her location has always been known. Veteran wreck diver Fred Rogers first visited the *Point Grey* during the spring of 1955. He described the wreck a lying partially submerged on its starboard beam and precariously balanced on Virago Rock. Fred and his dive buddy Pat Moloney swam into the wreck, and once inside, explored the compound steam engine and boiler room. He recorded that there were signs of earlier salvaging as the copper steam pipes had been sawn off down to the limit of the low tides, but otherwise the *Point Grey* was a virgin wreck, untouched after sinking.

During a winter storm in 1963, the wreck rolled off its perch on Virago Rock and settled upside down in 40 feet of water.

The UASBC visited the wreck on 13 December 1981 as part of its original Gulf Island project. The team found the wreck to be lying upside down in 45 feet of water southeast of the Virago Rock marker. The heavy steel hull was reported to be relatively intact except for some holes blasted amidships to facilitate the salvage of the engine. The divers also reported that they could swim unobstructed through most of the ship's length. They also reported that the propeller, minus one fluke (which lies off to the side), to still be in position. Additionally, they noted that the detached rudder lay on the bottom astern of the wreck.

An educational plaque was placed on the wreck of the *Point Grey* in 1983 per the recommendation in the 1982 report. The plaque was replaced in 1991 after vandals pried off the plexiglass panel, leaving behind the concrete base.

The UASBC dives the *Point Grey* wreck every couple of years. In 1991 we found that the wreck began to show increasing signs of deterioration. The bow had broken off from the stern and rolled right side up, while the stern remained upside down. One theory was that something hit the bow during low tide, causing it to break off. Another thought was that the holes blasted in the hull amidships may have compromised the structural integrity, combining with the strong current to break the hull apart.

Status

The UASBC visited the *Point Grey* on two occasions during the Gulf Islands re-inventory project, first on 17 October 2015 and again on 16 March 2019. During our second trip, we had planned to carry out photogrammetry to capture the essence of the wreck's three-dimensional stern. However, the underwater visibility on this trip was very poor (not more than 2 m) and we were unable to complete the photogrammetry. As such, the following description of the site will have to suffice.

The *Point Grey* is located on the southeast side Virago Rock in Porlier Pass. To find the wreck, you descend down the south side of the Virago Rock marker. When you reach the bottom, you will see a discarded navigation marker. Follow it down to the bottom and you will arrive on the fantail of the wreck. The wreck is located at 49° 00.760' N by 123° 35.563' W

The wreck measures 36.3 m long, oriented along a 052° heading (stern to bow) in two pieces. The stern lies upside down while the bow lies right-side-up. When diving the wreck, the first piece of wreckage encountered is the rudder, which lies astern of the fantail. The rudder measures 3.08 m long by 1.85 m wide. Forward of the rudder is the upside-down fantail of the wreck. 1.8 m forward of the fantail, is the rudder post. The steel propeller is 4 m forward of the stern, is still connected to the drive shaft and appears to hang in mid water. The length of each propeller blade is 1.1 m and they are connected to a 80-cm diameter hub. Only two blades remain attached to the hub. The third blade broke off at some point and now lies to the right of the fantail. The overall diameter of the propeller is about 3 m.

Diver examines two-bladed propeller on the *Point Grey*, courtesy of Dean Driver.

The stern section remains three-dimensional for a length of 15.6 m. The hull breaks at what would have been the divide between the engine room and boiler space. To the left of the break, lying against the reef is the large Scotch marine boiler. The boiler is 3.8 m long by 4.1 m in diameter and has two furnaces each 1.25 m in diameter. Looking back into the stern section at the break in the hull, one can see the drive shaft and the engine crank shaft. The remainder of the engine is missing.

Forward of the break in the hull is the bow section. As described earlier, it has rolled right-side-up and is deteriorating rapidly. The hull plating on the starboard side is still structurally intact. The port-side hull has completely collapsed in a jumble of frames and plating. An extant bulkhead is 22 m forward of the stern, with a second bulkhead is at 27.4 m. The wreckage ends 36.3 m from the stern at the stem post. The stem post has fallen to the port and now lies against the reef.

The depth at the stern was 34 feet (10.3 m) and the depth at the bow was 42 feet (12.8 m) on a 10.5-foot (3.2-m) tide.

Conclusions and Recommendations

The bow of the *Point Grey* is deteriorating rapidly and will undoubtedly collapse in the next few years. The stern has subsided somewhat, but is stable and remains in the shape of a ship. The propeller remains the single most attractive feature on this wreck and will offer sport divers a fascinating subject for photography for many years to come.

The *Point Grey* has an underwater interpretive plaque, still in reasonable condition, located at the stern of the wreck.

The UASBC does not have any new recommendations for this site.

References

J. S. Matthews Newspaper Collection, Point Grey, City of Vancouver Archives.

Cadieux Fonds, City of Vancouver Archives.

Clapp, Frank. *Ships of British Columbia Waters: An Illustrated History of Freighters, Ferries, Tankers, Trawlers and Tugs*, (Victoria, Nordnes Maritime Press, 2014).

Griffiths, David W. *A Report on the Historic Shipwrecks of the Southern Gulf Islands of British Columbia.* (Vancouver, unpublished, 1982), 162-167.

Mansbridge, Francis. *Launching History: The Saga of the Burrard Dry Dock*, (Madeira Park, Harbour Publishing, 2002).

Rogers, Fred. *Shipwrecks of British Columbia* (Vancouver, 1976), 25-28.

Vancouver Daily Province, 23 April 1949.

Ibid., 3 March 1949.

Ships Vertical File: Point Grey, Vancouver Maritime Museum.

Ship *Robert Kerr*

Ship *Robert Kerr* at Halifax Harbour, courtesy of W. R. MacAskill Nova Scotia Archives No. 1987-453 No.4883.

Official Number: 53862

Signal Letters: JHSL

Registry: Canada

Construction

Renowned Quebec City-based ship builder Narcisse Rosa began constructing the *Buffalo* in April 1865 at his shipyard on Hare Point, in St. Roche. He later renamed the vessel *Robert Kerr*, and launched it in May 1866. Measuring 190.6 feet long, 38.4 feet wide and 23.7 feet deep, the vessel displaced 1,911 gross tons and held a Lloyd's A1 designation. Rosa sheathed the hull with yellow metal and bestowed it with a female figurehead.

The vessel was ship-rigged and fitted with single top gallant and royals. Rosa used tamarack, oak, red and yellow pine and rock elm. An early survey reveals that, "this vessel's frame was built on stage and hoist up with double floors all fore and aft – keelsons are . . . bolted and clenched under keel – 17 pairs of crow plates 5 meters by 3/4 inches are fitted to outside of timber." Further, "three strakes 13 meters by 10 meters of rock elm, tamarac [sic] and red pine are worked over short floors head and futtock heels, well through and tie bolted." The "upper deck waterways are well fitted and bolted" and "lower deck clamps lower deck waterway are all well through bolted."

Rosa built the vessel for Robert Kerr and Sons, "merchants of Central Chambers," based in Liverpool. The owner of that firm named the vessel after himself.

Operational History

Robert Kerr initially sailed between Britain and Calcutta, India (present-day Kolkata). The firm likely retained commercial ties in that city as a previous family member, John Kerr, had resided there before his death in 1863. *Robert Kerr* made her first trip from Liverpool to Calcutta on 9 January 1867 under one Captain Hunter.

Hunter next sailed from Calcutta in July of 1867, arriving in New York City on 17 November. He returned to Liverpool, arriving on 27 January 1868. At some point thereafter, Hunter slipped Liverpool for Melbourne, Australia, arriving on 30 May. He left Melbourne on 9 July and loaded coal at Newcastle, eventually arriving in San Francisco on 6 November after a ninety-two-day transit. Hunter left San Francisco in January 1869 and arrived in Liverpool on 19 March. *Robert Kerr* later left

Liverpool and arrived in Melbourne on 8 October 1869. Hunter left Melbourne for San Francisco via Newcastle on 15 November, arriving on 20 March 1870. He left San Francisco for Liverpool on 15 April and arrived on 20 August. The vessel's owners removed *Robert Kerr* from Australian service, opting instead to have it visit Singapore. Hunter also turned over with one Captain McClure. *Robert Kerr's* movements between August of 1870 and December 1871 are unknown.

McClure departed Liverpool on 11 December 1871 and arrived in Singapore on 23 April 1872. He stayed in Singapore until 8 June, and then returned to Liverpool. *Robert Kerr's* movements during 1873 are unknown, but at some point, McClure turned over with a Captain Allen. Allen departed Liverpool on 1 May 1874 and arrived in Singapore on 8 August. Allen stayed in Singapore until 3 September, when he sailed for Rangoon (present-day Yangon). On 26 February 1875 Allen took *Robert Kerr* from Liverpool to Calcutta, returning later in the year.

Kerr sold the vessel to H. Fernie and sons in 1876. Interestingly, Kerr's eldest daughter Jessie had married into the Fernie family in August of 1863. *Robert Kerr's* movements are unknown until 22 April 1878, when it departed Calcutta for Boston under a Captain Fleming. The mysterious Captain Fleming committed suicide en route, requiring the crew to put into Cape Town on 4 June.

Robert Kerr eventually arrived at Boston on 1 August under a Captain Whittles. Whittles turned over with a Captain Pitt while alongside in Boston, and Pitt departed on 26 August. He sailed *Robert Kerr* to Galveston, where the crew found themselves quarantined for almost two months after arriving on 15 October. Authorities also surveyed the vessel at Galveston and they found it "entirely unseaworthy." Undaunted, Captain Pitt loaded 1,895 bales of cotton and sailed for Le Havre, France, on 11 December.

Robert Kerr eventually arrived back in Liverpool on 20 June 1879, after stopping in Saint John, New Brunswick. It sailed for New York in the second week of August and arrived in London under the command of a Captain Cowan on 15 November 1879. Cowan returned to New

York on 30 January 1880, and stayed until 16 April, when he sailed for Saint John. Shortly after leaving, the Philadelphia-bound steamer *A. O'Stimers* collided with *Robert Kerr* in heavy fog, carrying away the *Kerr*'s bobstay.

Robert Kerr arrived in Singapore from Liverpool on 24 November 1881, and left for Sandheads on 13 December. The vessel continued its blue-water service over the next few years, stopping in Liverpool, Rio de Janeiro, Newport, and throughout the American Pacific Northwest. *Robert Kerr* sailed from Europe for the last time on 1 October 1884 under a Captain Edward, bound for Panama. After a lengthy six-month crossing riddled with violence between crewmen and the death of Captain Edward, *Robert Kerr* finally arrived in Panama on 2 April 1885. The crew then sailed north to Victoria, and then from Victoria to Burrard Inlet, where they arrived near the end of September.

Next, they sailed for the San Juan Islands, but never completed the transit – while under tow and with a pilot onboard, they went aground near Lime Kiln, on San Juan Island. The crew successfully refloated the vessel two hours later, but found it was taking on four inches of water an hour. Insurance underwriters investigated the hull after the vessel's return to Vancouver. They decided that the severity of the damage rendered the vessel unseaworthy and scheduled an auction for 23 October 1885.

Local newspapers aggressively advertised the auction alongside advertisements announcing that the owners would not "be responsible for any debts contracted by the crew" – it seems the bellicose crew showed no signs of calming down. Among the men was Joe 'Seraphim' Fortes, who would later become a prominent figure in the history of early Vancouver. W. H. Soule, the superintendent of Vancouver's Hastings Mill, purchased the *Robert Kerr* for $1,000, instigating the next chapter of the vessel's life.

Soule intended to use *Robert Kerr* as a coal hulk to resupply vessels calling at the Hastings Mill. The overhaul was completed on 29 January 1886. Soule made a tidy profit three weeks later, when he sold the vessel to Robert Dunsmuir for $7,000. Dunsmuir kept the ship moored

Robert Kerr anchored in Burrard Inlet during fire of 1886, courtesy of UASBC Archives.

between Coal Harbour and the foot of Granville Street until October of 1886. It played and important role in events in Vancouver that summer. On 6 April 1886, "decorated in flags and bunting and ringing her bell the *Robert Kerr* took a prominent part in the official celebrations of the City's incorporation."

Next, on 13 June 1886, Canadian Pacific Railway (CPR) crews were engaged in the regular business of setting bush fires to clear land between present-day Cambie and Main streets, but a sudden strong gale caught the flames and rapidly spread them to the nearby structures, incinerating almost the entire ramshackle city in less than an hour. The gale blew *Robert Kerr* from its mooring off Deadman Island and east across the harbour, where the crew dropped anchor close to the shore just off the Hastings Mill, at the foot of Dunlevy Street. While some citizens dashed to the city's outskirts to escape the fire, others sought refuge in Burrard Inlet. Many took to makeshift rafts and made their way to the *Robert Kerr*, which eventually provided safe refuge to more than two hundred souls as the city burned.

Dunsmuir next had the hull surveyed in October 1886. After passing the survey, he immediately scheduled an auction for 28 October. The outcome of the survey is unknown, but by August 1887 the *Daily British Colonist* reported,

> a steam hoisting apparatus has been placed in the *Robert Kerr* at Vancouver and her dismantlement is now complete. Only the stumps of her mast and bowsprit are left and a large portion of her deck has been cut away for convenience in loading and unloading coal.

Robert Kerr thus became a coal hulk, and early British Columbian newspapers regularly reported on its movements throughout Southern Gulf Islands. Chandlers re-caulked, repainted and re-sheathed the hulk in Esquimalt, beginning on 18 April 1894 and finishing ten days later. Esquimalt-based chandlers replicated the effort at the end of February 1896. *Robert Kerr* spent twenty-four years as a coal hulk tirelessly servicing the CPR's fleet before being towed on it's final voyage.

Robert Kerr cut down to a barge at the Esquimalt Graving Dock, courtesy of UASBC Collection.

Loss

Robert Kerr's final voyage began from Ladysmith, where it had been loaded with 1,800 tons of coal destined for the RMS *Empress of India*, which the *Kerr* would meet in Vancouver. The tug *Coutil* buttoned onto the *Robert Kerr* on 5 March 1911, and it intended to transit to Vancouver via Porlier Pass. Disaster struck when *Coutil* accidentally towed *Robert Kerr* onto Danger Reef, just south of Miami Islet, while attempting to round Thetis Island. *Coutil* quickly removed the eight men onboard the hulk, but the now forty-five-year-old vessel did not fare well.

The *Daily British Colonist* reported that the vessel "filled quickly and lies partially submerged," had reportedly broken its back, "and was likely a total loss." A diver named James Moore travelled from Vancouver to survey the wreck, and reports quickly began making their way to Victoria. The CPR had insured the cargo of coal at $6,700. Moore reported that the fore hatch was above the waterline, and seemed confident that the coal could be salvaged.

Authorities reported that,

> the tug must have gone over the rock on which the *Kerr* struck and as the result of the impact a large hole has been torn in the bows of the *Robert Kerr*. The forepart is held in a cradle of rocks while the stern is imbedded in sand bottom. She is submerged from a little forward of amidships to aft, but the fore

hatch is clear. Thirty of feet of the false keel had been ripped off. Diver James Moore, who inspected the wreck, was able to walk under the hull, as it is hung at a sharp angle.

Shortly after the wreck the CPR posted watchmen nearby, as the Aboriginal population had made several enterprising forays to the site, making off with coal and the galley stove.

Salvage

Ten days after the *Kerr* grounded on Danger Reef, the CPR hired the Vancouver Wrecking and Salvage Company to retrieve the coal. The firm took station on the wreck with a tug and a dredger. The salvage outfit intended to use a suction pump to move the coal from the wreck onto a scow. Two weeks after the salvage began, the *Colonist* reported that between 1,200 and 1,300 tons

of coal had been removed from the wreck, along with the *Kerr*'s derricks and deck gear, but that the hull would be a total loss. The CPR responded to the wreck by purchasing the dismasted iron barque *Melanope* to replace the *Kerr*.

Search and Discovery

Nanaimo-based divers discovered the wreck of the *Robert Kerr* sometime in the late 1950s.

Gordon Squarebriggs of Nanaimo guided Fred Rogers and Ed Seton to the site in 1960. During his exploration, Fred recovered a number of large drift pins and Squarebriggs found a large slab of brass 1 inch thick and 8 inches wide. They presumed that it had been torn from the forefoot of the *Robert Kerr*. The whereabouts of these artifacts is unknown.

—Ralph Bower photo

ARTIFACTS, including a porcelain salt cellar, two spoons and black glass bottle, are displayed by diver Gord Esplin after being salvaged from sailing ship Robert Kerr, which sank off Thetis Island in 1911. Three-masted vessel was built in 1866. (Story, A8.)

Vancouver Sun article featuring UASBC divers on 10 May, 1982. Photo courtesy of Ralph Bower.

The UASBC visited the wreck site twice during its 1980-82 survey of Gulf Island wrecks. The first visit occurred on 24-25 April 1982, and the second visit 8-9 May 1982. During these early explorations, divers took photographs of the site and several small artifacts were raised and are visible in the newspaper article photo provided. They include a ceramic salt shaker, two spoons, and a bottle made of black glass. Additional artifacts; a bottle fragment, deck light, plate shard and shovel handle are stored in the UASBC collection.

When the *Robert Kerr* was converted from a ship to coal barge, several artifacts were removed and today can be found in the Vancouver Maritime Museum. These include its Union Jack ensign, logbook, telescope, and ship's bell.

Status

Archival records show that the UASBC has visited the *Robert Kerr* regularly since the release of the 1982 Gulf Islands report, in 1984, 1991, 1992, 2005, 2006, and 2009. On 4 March 2011, to commemorate the hundredth anniversary of the sinking, the UASBC put a new plaque on the *Robert Kerr* with the help of 49th Parallel Diving (Peter Luckham) and Andy Lamb from Cedar Beach Ocean Lodge.

The UASBC visited the *Robert Kerr* as part of the Gulf Islands re-inventory project over 7-9 April 2017 and on 24 February 2019, during which we logged 27 person-dives conducting a datum offset survey on the wreck and taking photos for photogrammetry.

The wreck lies in 8-18 m of water on the eastern slope of Danger Reef, midway between Miami Islet and the Ragged Islets off Pilkey Point on Thetis Island at 49° 02.022' N by 123° 42.303' W.

To survey the wreck site, divers ran a 60-m baseline from the sternpost to the bow area, identified by a single hawse pipe. The keel of the wreck is oriented along a 128° bearing stern to bow. The deepest point on the wreck is marked by a heavily degraded sternpost in 46.5 feet (14.2 m) of water recorded on a 7.8-foot (2.4-m) tide. The sternpost is also the starting location for the survey baseline. An iron capstan lies 3.5 m up the baseline and to the starboard side of the sternpost. It measures 70 cm in diameter by 1 m high. The

coal cargo begins 5 m up the baseline. A mound of coal covers the central portion of the wreck from the 5 metre mark to 30 metre mark on the baseline. The UASBC 2011 interpretation plaque lies 12 m up the baseline and 1 metre to port. At the 22.8-m mark, the rider keelson becomes visible protruding from beneath the coal. This heavy wood structure is 50 cm wide and it is flanked on either side with 20 cm planks, giving the keelson an overall width of 90 cm. When it sank, the *Kerr* settled on its starboard side, and so the keelson assembly is heavily canted to the starboard. The heavy starboard list has resulted in the port side being more exposed and more heavily damaged by marine borers. Some frames are visible 2.6 m from the keelson on the port side between the 18.4 m and 26 m distance along the baseline.

Between the 15 and 30m marks on the baseline and 6 m to starboard are a series of raised iron deck knees. These define the edge of the starboard hull, but the coal cargo spills well beyond the deck knee perimeter. The *Robert Kerr* was a composite-built vessel. It's wooden hull was reinforced with iron deck knees, which were used to fasten the frames to the deck beams. These right-angle shaped pieces of iron lie all over the wreck site and many of them are captured in the site survey.

A mast step is clearly visible on the rider keelson at 25.2 m. Given its position, this will be the main mast step. The extant hull rests on a rock ledge 34 m up the centreline. For years it was possible to swim under the suspended hull. The depth at this point is 6.6 m. The keelson deteriorates and breaks apart at 44 m. The baseline continues another 14 m before terminating at a lone hawse pipe at 58 m. The hawse pipe is 1.1 m long by 70 cm in diameter. Between the end of the keelson and the hawse pipe is a scattering of coal and iron knees on a smooth rounded rock bottom.

There are two artifacts that occur just outside the survey area. One object, a steel mast visible on the *Kerr* as a coal hulk, is located 12 m off the starboard side of the baseline at the 40-m mark. The top of the mast lies in 43.6 feet (13 .3 m) of water.

A second artifact that looks like the steering wheel boss lies on a ledge to the port side of the wreck.

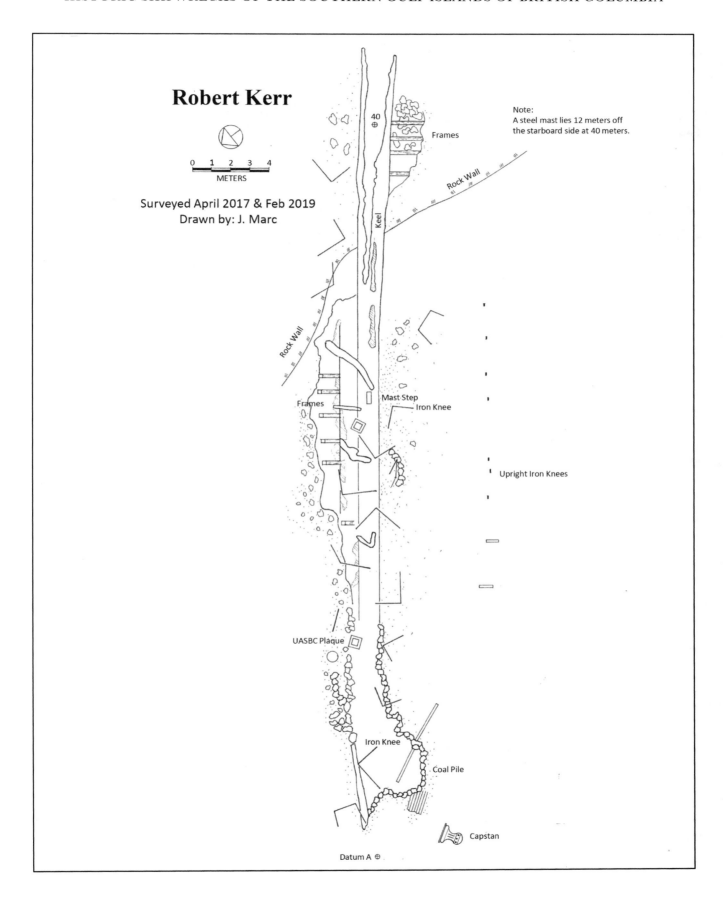

Robert Kerr

0 1 2 3 4
METERS

Surveyed April 2017 & Feb 2019
Drawn by: J. Marc

40

Frames

Note:
A steel mast lies 12 meters off
the starboard side at 40 meters.

Rock Wall

Keel

Rock Wall

Frames

Mast Step
Iron Knee

Upright Iron Knees

UASBC Plaque

Iron Knee

Coal Pile

Capstan

Datum A

A diver hovers above wheel boss.
(Ewan Anderson Photo)

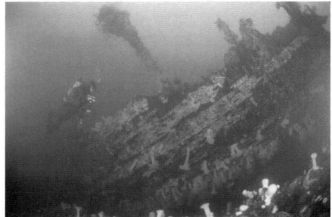

A diver surveys extant starboard hull in 1982
(Neil McDaniel Photo)

Conclusions/Recommendations

Unlike *Miami*, the *Robert Kerr* is still routinely visited by sport divers. In the 1990s, the wreck was somewhat intact and it was possible to swim under the suspended hull. Today, thirty years later, the elements have taken their toll. The wooden hull and frames are almost gone and the keelson is slowly collapsing in on itself from the weight of the coal cargo. Despite the ongoing deterioration of the woodwork on the wreck, there are still many features such as the capstan, mast, hawse pipe and wheel boss to look at and make this a worthwhile dive. The UASBC educational plaque put on site in 2011 is still in good condition and is not in immediate need of replacement.

Many of the small artifacts noted in the stern area in the 1982 report (e.g. coal shovels, crockery, intact stern house windows, and black glass bottles) are long gone. The larger artifacts are not something that the average diver will want to recover. As such, the *Heritage Conservation Act* provides adequate protection for what is left on this wreck.

References

Boston Daily Advertiser, 9 August 1867.

Ibid., 19 November 1867.

Ibid.,13 February 1868.

Ibid., 21 March 1870.

Ibid., 18 April 1870.

Ibid., 22 April 1878.

Ibid., 27 August 1878.

Ibid.,18 November 1879.

Daily Evening Bulletin, 7 November 1868.

Ibid., 19 February 1870.

Ibid., 21 September 1870.

Ibid., 22 April 1885.

Ibid., 27 February 1886.

Daily Southern Cross, Vol. XXIV, 17 June 1868.

Gulf Islands Driftwood, 1 November 1983.

Griffiths, David W. *A Report on the Historic Shipwrecks of the Southern Gulf Islands of British Columbia.* (Vancouver, unpublished, 1982),

Robert Kerr, letter from Merseyside County Council, 17 May 1983.

Rogers, Fred. *Shipwrecks of British Columbia* (Vancouver, 1976), 47-48.

Rogers, Fred. *Historic Divers of British Columbia – A History of Hardhat Diving, Salvage and Underwater Construction*, (Duncan: Firgrove Publishing, 2003), 73-74.

Straits Times Overland Journal, 5 April 1872.

Ibid., 5 September 1874.

Ibid., 8 August 1874.

Ibid., 19 December 1881.

The Daily British Colonist, 10 September 1885.

Ibid., 3 October 1885.

Ibid., 26 August 1885.

Ibid., 25 October 1885.

Ibid., 29 January 1886.

Ibid., 14 February 1886.

Ibid., 1 October 1886.

Ibid., 28 August 1887.

Ibid., 18 April 1894.

Ibid., 28 April 1894.

Ibid., 29 February 1896.

Ibid., 7 March 1911.

Ibid., 8 March 1911.

Ibid., 9 March 1911.

Ibid., 10 March 1911.

Ibid., 15 March 1911.

Ibid., 1 April 1911.

Ibid., 7 April 1911.

The Galveston Daily News, 12 December 1878.

The North American, 29 November 1878.

Ibid., 31 January 1880.

Ibid., 17 April 1880.

The Times, 11 January 1867.

Ibid., 27 February 1875.

Ibid., 23 June 1879.

Ibid., 26 November 1881.

UASBC File: *Robert Kerr*, 'The Ship That Saved Vancouver.

UASBC File: *Robert Kerr*, Public Archives of Canada, Microfilm A-477, No. 770.

UASBC File: Robert Kerr, Agreement and Account of Crew. 29 September 1884.

Ship *John Rosenfeld*

Ship *John Rosenfeld* taking shape on the ways of E. & A. Sewall in 1883, courtesy of UASBC Archives.

Official Number: 76506

Signal Letters: KCNL

Registry: United States

Construction

Maine's prolific shipbuilder E. & A. Sewall began gathering materials for the *John Rosenfeld* in July of 1883, and began construction later that fall. Sewall relied on Portland's Rufus Deering & Company and the nearby William S. Hunt lumber merchants for well over 10,000 feet of pine, spruce, and white wood. Boston's A. L. Cutler & Company supplied varnishes beginning in October, James E. Haley supplied sheathing, and Bath's own Swanton, Jameson & Company chandler provided a significant volume of odds and ends. The vessel that slowly took form in the Sewall yard eventually measured 256.5 feet long, 44 feet wide, and 28.6 feet deep. The recorded gross tonnage was 2,374, or 2,268 net, and the *Rosenfeld* sported the official number of 76506.

The ship was named after prominent San Francisco merchant John Rosenfeld, who owned a one-eighth interest along with the vessel's only captain, James G. Baker, while Sewall owned the other six shares.

According to respected maritime historian Frederick C. Matthews, the *Rosenfeld* "was a superior vessel in model and finish and very strongly constructed. From the top of the keelson to the bottom of the keel there was 12 feet of solid timber. The cabins were built in palace car style and finished throughout with solid cherry, polished."

The *Rosenfeld* cost an impressive $150,000, "and was launched by the bright light of the moon on June 21, 1884, with masts all set up and rigging nearly complete."

Operational History

John Rosenfeld's working life began shortly after its launch, first appearing in New York City on 14 July 1884, and then in Baltimore two weeks later, on 28 July. It sailed from Baltimore for San Francisco laden with 3,585 tons of coal on 11 August. Irons initially hampered the trip, and it took the crew forty-two days to reach the equator. They finally arrived at their destination after a transit that took the remainder of 1884, arriving in San Francisco on 3 January 1885. The crew had a brief but welcome rest for four days, and then loaded wheat on 7 January in San Francisco. *Rosenfeld* then sailed from San Francisco to Liverpool, arriving towards the end of June and making a return transit to San Francisco on 1 July 1885, arriving in November of that year. The crew spent four days weathering a severe storm that prevented access to San Francisco's harbour, losing their fore and main yards in the process. The *Rosenfeld* sailed from San Francisco for the last time on 7 January 1886, setting in motion the events leading to its destruction – a mere twenty months after its launch.

Loss

The *Rosenfeld* arrived in Nanaimo on 24 January 1886, and began loading coal sometime thereafter. Captain Baker weighed anchor at 20:00 on 18 February, at which point the steam tug *Tacoma* secured a 600-foot towing hawser to the *Rosenfeld's* port side and the two ships departed Nanaimo Harbour. Baker noted "pleasant weather and light north-westerly airs," and that at 22:00 "passed outside of Gabriola Reef, and proceeded down the fairway of the straits of Georgia . . . passed Active Pass light at five miles distant."

The two vessels continued south intending to round East Point and enter Boundary Pass, but at 04:45 on 19 February the *Rosenfeld* "struck heavily on a reef off Tumbo Island and slid up the reef at the top of high water and remained stationary." The *Tacoma's* crew then released the hawser to allow the tug to come alongside the stricken *Rosenfeld*. Baker asked John H. Cameron, the tug's skipper, if they could make Port Townsend before the next high tide, to which Cameron replied that they could not. The crews then unloaded personal baggage from the *Rosenfeld* onto the *Tacoma*, and heaved as much coal overboard as they could in an attempt to lighten the grounded ship. The tug made its hawsers fast to the *Rosenfeld's* stern and tried to free it during the next high tide, but the crews' efforts were to no avail.

Baker then dispatched the *Tacoma* to Port Townsend to seek assistance, "with orders to return as quickly as possible" while the shipwrecked crew remained in place. These men continued to "heave overboard more coal, and so continued until about 11 o'clock PM of the 19th February, when ship suddenly fell over to starboard, bilged and soon filled with water." The crew took to the lifeboats, which maintained a lonely vigil on the wreck until the next morning.

Salvage

The *Tacoma* returned and came alongside the wreck at 09:00 on 20 February, and the men commenced putting "all ships lines, stores and other things such as sails, cabin furniture, lights and part of crew aboard" before Baker dispatched the tug back to Port Townsend. He then "commenced to wreck ship with remains of crew and continued until 6 PM then went ashore and camped on the beach."

The following morning saw the *Tacoma* back alongside the wreck with a scow, which the men loaded with anchors and chains. The Victoria-based tug *Alexander* also attempted to free the *Rosenfeld* at some point during the evening of 20 February, without success. The salvage on 21 February lasted until 17:00, when the crew "put all movable wreckage aboard the tug" and Baker once again dispatched it to Port Townsend.

On 22 February, Baker recorded that the men "continued to wreck ship throughout the day, starboard rail under water when we left ship," while his summary for 23 February merely reads "continued to wreck ship all day." At 17:00 on 24 February the schooner *Mary Parker* came alongside the wreck, which the men loaded with salvage.

Baker recorded that by 25 February the men "finished wrecking ship of all except standing rigging. Loaded it aboard schooner and left ship (leaving one man aboard) for Port Townsend."

The *Parker* arrived at its destination on 26 February, and on 27 February Baker "chartered steam tug *Virginia* and left about 10AM, with eight men and necessary tools to get standing rigging from ship." The salvage party reached the wreck site at 18:00 the same day, but heavy seas prevented them from getting aboard. The crew worked from dawn until dusk on 28 February. The men began at daylight the next day, and at 07:00 the *Mary Parker* once again took station on the wreck. The salvage party worked until noon, "when we knocked off, that being the time of the sale of the ship and cargo at Victoria."

The following day, 2 March, the *Mary Parker* set sail for Port Townsend, although not before Victoria's Mr. C. Hayward, the new owner of the *Rosenfeld* and its remaining cargo, took possession at the wreck site. He quickly saw to unloading the coal into lighters, and by 9 March even the intrepid Vancouver-based *Beaver* was engaged in the salvage. By 17 March, Hayward began auctioning off the Rosenfeld's cargo at Victoria's Janion Wharf.

View down *John Rosenfeld*'s deck, tug *Tacoma* in background, courtesy of UASBC Archives.

Beginning in November 1886, a lengthy legal battle followed the events surrounding the *Rosenfeld*'s wrecking, during which the particulars of the accident came to light. Baker made a brief stop at Port Angeles on 21 January before arriving at Nanaimo, where he arranged for the *Tacoma* to meet and tow him to open water for $600. Interestingly, Sewall refused to employ Canadian

tugs after another company ship, *Thrasher*, wrecked near Gabriola Reef on the rock now bearing that vessel's name.

The court minutes reveal that "the water was calm, the night clear, and the points, headlands and shore could be plainly seen from the tug," but

> that up to within about fifteen minutes of the stranding the tug and tow were proceeding on nearly an east south east course in a safe channel, but had not as yet reached the point where it was usual and ordinary for vessels to turn in order to enter Haro Straits, but were in fact a mile or more west, and a considerable distance north of said usual line, or turning point which fact the officers in charge of said tug ought to have known and could have ascertained by the use of his eyes and compass.

In other words, the *Tacoma*'s crew tried to cut the corner around East Point and the *Rosenfeld*, with her considerably deeper draft, didn't clear the reef that the tug steamed over. However, the court also found that Baker

> without examination to ascertain the character or extent of the injury to the ship and without any reasonable cause for doing so and knowing she was a new and strong ship and only slightly injured, recklessly determined to abandon her, and did in fact abandon and commence wrecking her without cause.

The judge eventually ordered that George E. Atkinson, the *Tacoma*'s owner, pay $12,500 to Sewall, a mere fraction of the vessel's original $150,000 cost and $26,000 cargo.

Search and Discovery

Rosenfeld Rock is part of a large reef system that extends from the southern tip of Tumbo Island out to the green marker buoy U59. The rock lies in a very exposed location. The currents can reach 5-6 knots and strong southeast winds make diving at this location a challenge.

Author and diver Fred Rogers recorded two attempts

to locate the *Rosenfeld* in his book *Shipwrecks of British Columbia*. His first attempt was 13 September 1962. He recounted that the team didn't have a depth sounder, so they searched for the reef using a sounding lead. Eventually he found the wreck when the current went slack and kelp came to the surface. During his dives he found a few brass pins and some pieces of oxidized iron in a gully in 30 feet of water. Unfortunately, he does not provide any information as to where the gully was in relation to the reef. He visited the site a second time on 15 August 1967, at which time he again located the gully, but did not find any additional wreckage.

On 18-20 December 1981, the UASBC undertook the first of a number of planned search operations for the remains of the *John Rosenfeld* wreck. Six person-dives were completed on 19 December, finding some copper sheathing and coal off the southeast corner of the reef. Unfortunately, on 20 December the weather deteriorated, forcing the UASBC to abandon further searches at the site.

On 18-19 September 1982, a small party of UASBC divers aboard the MV *Compass Rose* completed three additional dives at Rosenfeld Rock. On the second dive, David Griffiths and Dennis Ward were exploring a gully on the Georgia Strait (north) side of the reef at a depth of 55 feet when they discovered a large amount of heavily concreted anchor chain running up the wall of the gully and up on to the reef. They also found a considerable amount of copper sheathing on top of the reef in 27 feet (8.2 m) of water.

On Sunday, 19 December, more dives explored the gully area. At a depth of 30 feet (8.3 m), the divers found that the bottom changed from smooth, sculpted sandstone to scattered boulders. Upon closer examination, the boulders turned out to be large pieces of coal. Near the gully, divers also found two brass drift pins in 35 feet (10.6 m) of water. They recovered a few pieces of coal and the pins for further study.

The UASBC has attempted to dive Rosenfeld Rock three times in recent years. On 23 August 2008, UASBC divers found the reef and spent time diving on its north side, as that was where the UASBC had found material in 1982.

The top of the reef was in 26 feet (7.9 m) of water on a 10.6-foot tide. Very little material was found on the north side aside from the occasional drift bolt wedged in rock crevices.

Near the end of their dive, UASBC divers moved across to the south side of the reef and began finding debris. We returned to the site on 30 August 2009 and dived on the coordinates where the 2008 dive ended, focusing on the south slope of the reef. On this dive, we found a depression full of ship artifacts in 35 feet (10.6 m) of water. The coordinates were 48° 48.108' N by 123° 02.370' W. There were deck knees, a bollard, a parrel, a mooring port and chain plates. A second team found a major chunk of ship hull further to the south in 60 feet (18.2 m) of water. Time did not permit any measurements as the current had changed. On 3 September 2011, the UASBC returned to the site to further explore the area and measure the hull segment. On this occasion the current did not go slack and the dive was cancelled.

Status

The UASBC is convinced that the wreckage found is from the *Rosenfeld*, as no other major wooden ship was lost here. The large sizes of the brass drift-bolts also indicate a 200-foot vessel. We believe that that the main body of the wreck must have been gradually broken up by wind, wave, and current action, scattering the wreckage. The side walls and superstructure would have broken off and floated away, while the lower hull would have remained on the reef for some time. However, eventually the lower hull would have been weakened by rot and marine borers. Over time, the strong currents would have pulled it apart, with some pieces remaining on the reef and other pieces carried into deeper water.

Conclusions/Recommendations

Despite UASBC efforts, the true extent of the *Rosenfeld* wreck site remains unknown. Our only recommendation for this site is that additional searches be undertaken at Rosenfeld Rock to determine if more of the wreck exists.

References

Daily Alta California, 29 May 1884.

Ibid., 16 July 1884.

Ibid., 1 August 1884.

Ibid., 16 August 1884.

Ibid., 3 January 1885.

Ibid., 18 August 1885.

Daily British Colonist, 24 February 1886

Ibid., 21 February 1886.

Ibid., 10 March 1886.

Ibid., 26 October 1886.

Frederick C. Matthews. *American Merchant Ships: 1850-1900*, (Salem: Marine Research Society, 1930), 186.

Griffiths, David W. *A Report on the Historic Shipwrecks of the Southern Gulf Islands of British Columbia.* (Vancouver, unpublished, 1982), 23-34.

Maine Maritime Museum, MS 22, Box 357, Folder 3.

Maine Maritime Museum, MS 22, Box 357, Folder 4.

Maine Maritime Museum, MS 22, Box 457, Folder 3.

Rogers, Fred. *Shipwrecks of British Columbia* (Vancouver, 1976), 86-87.

Rowe, William. *The Maritime History of Maine: Three Centuries of Shipbuilding and Seafaring*, (New York: W.W. Norton & Company, 1948), 213.

Ship *Thrasher*

Full-rigged ship *Gatherer* (sister ship to *Thrasher*) clearing Delaware. Painting by Alexander Charles Stuart, courtesy of Vallejo Galleries.

Official Number: 145110

Signal Letters: JRTV

Registry: United States

Construction

The prominent New England shipbuilding firm of E. & A. Sewall built *Thrasher* during the winter and summer of 1876, and launched it on 1 July of that year. Shipwright Elisha P. Mallett designed *Thrasher* as a two-deck vessel, square-rigged on all three masts. Mallet used hackmatack, oak, yellow pine, and hemlock, fastened with copper bolts and sheathed with yellow metal. *Thrasher* was 211 feet 9 inches long, 39 feet 7 inches wide, with a 24-foot draft, and it displaced 1512 tons. The American government issued *Thrasher* the Official Number 145110 and Signal Letters JRTV.

To give underwriters and merchants an idea of the condition of the vessels they insured and chartered, Lloyd's Register graded ship hulls on a lettered scale (A being the best), and ship's fittings (masts, rigging, and other equipment) on a numbered scale (1 being the best). Thus, the best classification was "A1." Lloyd's assigned *Thrasher* an A1 rating.

Located in Bath, Maine, the Sewall family's yard was one of the most prolific in the American Northeast. Mallett relied on models rather than plans, but historians can safely assume that the workers who toiled to build *Thrasher* did so with decades of knowledge at their disposal – starting with its first ship in 1823, by 1903 the Sewall yard had launched 150 vessels, "all on their own account and known around the world."

Operational History

The Sewalls not only built the *Thrasher*, but they owned it up until it wrecked on Gabriola Reef. *Thrasher* was a four-year-old vessel classed A1 and valued at $100,000 at the time of its loss. Captain Robert Bosworth, the vessel's master, had a $12,000 share in the ship.

Bosworth took command of *Thrasher* after its launch in 1876, and retained that role until its loss four years later. Despite *Thrasher*'s short lifespan, Bosworth sailed it around the world. On 26 July 1876, he called at Baltimore, slipping on 4 August, and after a 160-day transit, he made San Francisco on 15 January 1877 laden with 2,225 tons of coal. Bosworth remained there until 9 March, when he sailed for Queenstown, United Kingdom, arriving in July. *Thrasher* next sailed to Liverpool in the same month, where it arrived September.

Next, Bosworth sailed for Rangoon (present-day Yangon), Burma, making that port by 15 January 1878. Bosworth spent the following two years industriously – he sailed from Rangoon back to Liverpool, where the ship retained its A1 rating. Following that, it then went to Calcutta (present-day Kolkata), Falmouth, and Dundee, finally stopping in New York at some point in September of 1879.

Bosworth spent most of the fall loading cargo, and slipped New York for San Francisco on 10 December laden with 1,512 tons of cargo. *Thrasher* arrived in San Francisco in April 1880. It sailed from that city for Nanaimo in May, and reached its destination in June. Bosworth then engaged in shipping coal over June and July, when disaster struck. The Sewall firm clearly trusted Bosworth – once the *Thrasher* left Maine, it sailed for four years without returning.

Loss

Historians are particularly lucky that Captain Bosworth's statement on *Thrasher*'s loss survives in the Maine Maritime Museum. He declared that on the evening of Wednesday, 14 July 1880, the vessel took on 2,466 tons of coal at Nanaimo, with the intended destination of San Francisco. The tugs *Etta White* and *Beaver* fastened hawsers onto the *Thrasher* at the jetty in Nanaimo, and proceeded to sail in clear weather with light airs. Bosworth later testified that he wanted a more powerful tug, but could not locate one.

At 20:30, the tugs accidentally

> struck on what's called Gabriola Reef, with a shock that shook the ship from stem to stern. The hand-lead showed but 16 feet of water under her bow – sounded the pumps and found the ship taking water rapidly. A hawser was run astern to the tugs and made ready to attempt to tow the ship into deep water, but finding she was making water so rapidly it was deemed imprudent to move her.

The incident took place at high tide, and by slack water at 03:00, "she listed over to starboard and rested her bilge on the bottom," completely flooded.

The next day, the crew transferred the sails and rigging to the *Beaver*, and on 16 July they "continued stripping the ship of all moveables of value, such as sails, ropes, blocks, anchors, chains, etc." Bosworth left the wreck on 16 July and travelled to Victoria via Nanaimo on the *Etta White*, "and with the U.S. Consul, visited Admiral Stirling, of Her Majesty's Ship *Triumph*, laying the situation of the ship before him and soliciting aid, which was promptly offered." The following two days the crew "continued lightening the ship of all moveables."

On 19 July,

> the tug *Etta White* having in tow a barge containing two steam pumps and diving apparatus in company with the British Gun Boat *Rocket* arrived. Work was immediately commenced to lighten the ship by throwing overboard the coal cargo, assisted by the hoisting boat *Lilly*, and putting the steam pumps at work to free the ship of water. The divers, at the same time, were at work stopping as far as possible the holes from the outside.

A diver from *HMS Triumph* discovered the ship's forefoot and keel planking torn off for a distance of 10 feet.

Over the following two days, everyone present "used every means at hand to lighten the ship and free her of water, but all efforts were fruitless." Divers repaired some of the underwater damage, but the pumps failed to cope with the amount of water in the hold. On 22 July, Bosworth dismissed the *Lilly* to Nanaimo, laden with much of the *Thrasher*'s movables. Between 23-26 July heavy weather ceased the salvage operation, by which point "the ship has worked, and strained very much during the last three days, besides having her houses destroyed, and other damages." The weather calmed on 27 July, when "all the people belonging to the ship except the second mate and four seamen were brought to Nanaimo, V.I., our port of departure."

A protracted legal battle between Sewall and the tugging company followed the wrecking incident. In 1881 Victoria's infamous judge Matthew Begbie found the tugs innocent of any wrongdoing on the grounds that Bosworth did not specifically seek out a pilot, but instead took for granted that the tug captains possessed knowledge of pilotage waters, and that Bosworth retained command and charge of the flotilla. Nevertheless, the case finally ended in the Supreme Court of Canada in Sewall's favour.

Salvage

The rigging, sails and other material salvaged from *Thrasher* immediately after the wrecking were loaded onto the sailing ship *Challenger*, which sailed for San Francisco on 31 July 1880. The sails and equipment fetched $3,400 at auction.

Declaring the wreck a total loss, Sewall put it up for auction. On 31 July 1808, Mr. J. F. Engelhardt bought Thrasher for $500 at a public auction facilitated by Messrs W. R. Clarke & Company. The cargo, consisting of 2,400 tons of Wellington coal, was knocked down to the same bidder at $50.

The wreck was re-sold to C. W. Horth for $520 on 5 August 1880. The salvage began in the second week of August, and it is presumed that the salvers focused on recovering the cargo of coal, as they ultimately abandoned the hull. The 18 September edition of the *Colonist* describes the *Thrasher* as being in the same position as when it wrecked, with lower masts and lower rigging standing. It further specifies, "all the top gear has been removed and when northwest winds prevail, the sea breaks clean over the wreck. The wrecking party have relinquished work for the present."

A report one year later on 20 November 1881 describes the wreck as appearing much broken up, with one of the masts carried away and the other two greatly out of position.

It would appear the plight of the *Thrasher* generated a bit of a tourism opportunity. On Thursday, 5 August, the steamer *Cariboo-Fly* took 80 passengers from Nanaimo to the ship *Thrasher*, wrecked off Gabriola Reef.

Search and Discovery

In 1959, a group of Vancouver Island and Gulf Island divers searched for the *Thrasher* and recovered an iron bollard.

During the summer of 1963, veteran wreck diver Fred Rogers and Bill Bernard dived the wreck and recovered some lead sheathing, most likely left behind by the salvage divers in 1880.

Fred Rogers with lead sheathing recovered from the *Thrasher* wreck, courtesy of Vancouver maritime Museum Collection.

The UASBC searched for the wreck during its Gulf Islands project in 1982. We found parts of the wreck in 30-50 feet of water north and northeast of Thrasher Rock. The remains consist of a few battered and scattered timbers and portions of anchor chain. The remains of the iron capstan/windlass drum lie in 45 feet of water northeast of the marker, and a quantity of coal still remains.

Status

UASBC Explorations Director, Jacques Marc, visited the wreck on 6 October 1986. During his visit he recorded that some of the remains were still visible in 60 feet of water 150 m northeast of the marker. The main body of the wreck lies buried on a flat sandy bottom. Only rows of bronze spikes and drift pins mark the location of what once were hardwood timbers. Protruding from the sand are deadeyes heavily encrusted with marine growth, showing the wreck is that of a once proud sailing vessel. Near the stern of the wreck lie three bronze sternpost gudgeons barely corroded after 106 years beneath the sea.

Much of what appears to be barnacle-encrusted rock surrounding the wreck is actually part of the *Thrasher*'s cargo.

The rudder gudgeons documented in 1986 were recovered in the late 1980s by a commercial diver when harvesting geoduck clams in the area.

The UASBC travelled to the site on 17 June 2017. However, muddy water from Fraser River, rough seas and strong currents thwarted our efforts to dive the site.

The UASBC tried again on 23 September 2018. On this trip the seas were calm and the current was slack. Ten person-dives found a substantial amount of material on site. The Thrasher Rock navigational marker lies at coordinates 49 08 59.9 N 123 38 29.6 W. It was used as a datum point to reference our finds.

Diver with unknown metal support brackets. Photo courtesy of Ewan Anderson.

An extensive search found that the wreckage was concentrated in two areas. Extant hull material, a large concentration of anchor chain, large pieces of coal and a lifeboat davit were located 87 m at 353° from the day marker in 11 m (35 feet) of water on a 1.5 m (4.9-foot) tide. Divers found a second grouping of artifacts 213 m at 36° from

the marker in 18 m (60 feet) of water.

The hull remnant is oriented roughly along a –northeast-southeast line, and measured 35 m long with an average width of 2.5 m. Along the eastern side of the hull piece are three distinct clumps of chain plates. In some cases, the chain plates were topped with iron hoops still containing lignum vitae deadeyes. At the southern end of the hull is a possible naval pipe. This is a through-deck iron fitting flanged on top that allowed the anchor chain to drop below decks into the chain locker after coming up the hawse pipe and through the windlass. Near the naval pipe are some metal features that appear to be support brackets. Initial speculation was that they may have supported the windlass. However, the construction of these pieces does not appear robust enough to support a piece of equipment as substantial as a windlass. Large quantities of coal are scattered near the hull piece.

Divers did not find the capstan reported to be on site in the early 1980s.

Conclusions and Recommendations

Given the dispersed nature of the *Thrasher* remains and the low diver visitation, the UASBC has no recommendations for this site. The rock that ended the *Thrasher*'s career is now marked with a navigation marker, and so no interpretive plaque is necessary.

References

American Lloyd's Register of American and Foreign Shipping, 1877, 1878, 1879, 1880.

Bangor Daily Whig and Courier, 3 July 1876.

Daily Alta California, 27 July 1876.

Ibid., 11 December 1879.

Daily British Colonist, July 16, 1880.

Ibid., 17 July 1880.

Ibid., 25 July 1880.

Ibid., 31 July 1880.

Ibid., 1 August 1880.

Ibid., 7 August 1880.

Ibid., 11 August 1880.

Ibid., 12 September 1880.

Ibid., 18 September 1880.

Ibid., 30 June 1881.

Ibid., 20 November 1881.

Daily Evening Bulletin, 16 January 1877.

Diver Magazine, March 1987.

Griffiths, David W. *A Report on the Historic Shipwrecks of the Southern Gulf Islands of British Columbia*. (Vancouver, unpublished, 1982), 176-180.

Maine Maritime Museum, MS-22 Sewall Family Papers 1761-1965 Series II Vessel Papers Entry 497 Thrasher (ship) Voyages 1876-1880, Hull 8.

Record of American and Foreign Shipping, 1877, 1878, 1879 and 1881.

Rogers, Fred. *Shipwrecks of British Columbia*, (Vancouver: J. J. Douglas Ltd., 1976), 65-66.

Rogers, Fred. *Historic Divers of British Columbia – A History of Hardhat Diving, Salvage and Underwater Construction*, (Duncan: Firgrove Publishing, 2003), 26, 34.

Rowe, William. *The Maritime History of Maine: Three Centuries of Shipbuilding and Seafaring*, (New York: W. W. Norton & Company, 1948).

Wright, E. W., ed. *Lewis & Dryden's Marine History of the Pacific Northwest*, (New York: Antiquarian Press, Ltd., 1961), 280.

http://gabriolahistory.ca/placenames/Thrasher.pdf

Barque *Zephyr*

The American Clipper Barque *Zephyr* in Messina Harbour, Sicily 1856. Painting by William Bygrave, courtesy of UASBC Collection.

Official Number: None

Registry: United States

Construction

The renowned Medford, Massachusetts-based shipyard of Hayden and Cudworth launched the *Zephyr* on 18 August 1855. The ship had one deck, three masts, and was 125 feet long, 28 feet 4 inches wide, and 12 feet 10.5 inches deep. The builders designed her as a 414-ton barque with a proud stern, no galleries, and an unrecorded figurehead for Sylvester K. Small of Boston. Born in 1822, Small spent forty-one years at sea – twenty-eight of them as a Master Mariner – before marrying in 1844 and finally opening "the Travelers Home" in 1884 in Chatham, Massachusetts.

Hayden and Cudworth are principally remembered for being a leader in building clipper ships, having launched thirty-nine such ships between 1850 and 1856. Elisha Hayden and William Cudworth both hailed from the Sea View area of Marshfield, Massachusetts, and went into business together on the former yard of Thatcher Magoun in 1846. Both men listed their profession as carpenters in the 1850 federal census. By 1860, both held respectable estates, and after twenty years in business, they closed their yard in 1866.

Operational History

Small lost no time making a return on his investment, sailing from Boston on 10 September 1855 for Constantinople (present-day Istanbul), Turkey, arriving on 12 November. He then sailed for the Italian city of Messina on 30 November, arriving on 4 January 1856 and sailing for Boston eight days later, reporting at Gibraltar on 1 February and arriving at his destination on 25 April. Small then transited south to Savannah, arriving on 10 May before sailing for Sydney, Australia, on 30 May. *Zephyr* arrived in Sydney on 21 September, and sailed for Singapore on the same day. Small arrived in Singapore towards the end of 1856, and sailed for Boston on 12 January 1857, making Boston on 2 May. *Zephyr* next sailed for Gibraltar on 5 June, arriving on 1 July and then sailing through the Mediterranean to Trieste, Italy, arriving on 2 August. Small then sailed south to Beirut, Lebanon, before heading east to Boston from that port on 19 September, clearing Gibraltar on 27 October and arriving 30 November 1857.

Small ushered in 1858 by sailing from Boston on 15 January for Valparaiso, Chile, arriving on 27 April. At some point between then and 30 June *Zephyr* sailed to Caldera, a port city in northern Chile, before returning to Boston on 28 January 1859. Small next sailed from Boston in February and visited Algoa Bay, South Africa, on 10 April. He quickly returned to Boston, but sailed for Archangel (Arkhangelsk), Russia, on 13 May and arrived on 26 June, before sailing for Boston on 24 July. After returning to Boston, Small sailed for "Gibraltar and a market" on 22 October. Small and his crew experienced "heavy weather with westerly winds, nearly all passage" and eventually called at Marseilles on 6 December.

Small then sailed to Messina on 17 December, and arrived six days later. The crew must have enjoyed an Italian Christmas and New Year's before sailing for Boston on 7 January 1860. Fellow mariners first observed Small on 20 January at Cabo de Gatt, off the Iberian coast, and he called at Gibraltar on 4 February before finally arriving in Boston on 7 March. On 4 April, *Zephyr* sailed for Valparaiso – its third trip around Cape Horn – and arrived by 17 July. Next, on 3 August Small sailed north to Arica, Chile, and arrived on 22 August. *Zephyr* continued north to Pisagua, Peru, where it stopped on 23 September before returning to Boston on 3 January 1861.

Small next sailed for Wilmington, North Carolina, on 26 January 1861 and arrived on 4 February. After a brief stay, Small cleared Wilmington for Liverpool on 2 March, arriving on 29 March. He sailed from there to Gibraltar, arriving on 16 May but quickly reversed course north to Cadiz, where he loaded cargo and then cleared that port for Buenos Aries on 22 July. After a brief stop in New York in mid-October, Small turned up in Bermuda on 21 October, where he spent three days before reportedly sailing for Livorno, Italy.

However, it seems that Small turned east again, putting in at New York and turning over with one Captain Howes, who departed on 7 November, briefly stopping at Messina on 19 January 1862. Howes then cleared Messina for Philadelphia – apparently not proceeding to Livorno – on 1 February, and arrived near the end of March. Small met him in Philadelphia, where he once again took *Zephyr*'s helm and set sail for Dublin on 29 March, arriving on 11 June and then sailing further east through the Mediterranean for Genoa, putting in on 27 July. Small departed Genoa shortly thereafter, briefly stopping at Alicante and calling at Gibraltar on 14 September before crossing the Atlantic and arriving in New York on 18 October.

On 29 November, Small cleared New York for Malaga, Spain, and arrived on 1 January 1863, but then sailed into the now-familiar port of Messina on 3 February, staying three nights before setting out for New York. Small weathered heavy gales in the mid-Atlantic and sprung his foremast, limping into New York Harbor on 9 April. While there, Small again turned over with Howes, who cleared New York for Cadiz on 9 May, but turned up in Malaga on 7 June and finally back in New York on 2 August. Howes turned over *Zephyr* to Small shortly after his arrival in New York, and Small sailed north to Boston on 12 August, arriving six days later. *Zephyr* remained alongside Boston until 7 October, when Small again sailed east to Marseilles, arriving on 17 November. Small then sailed for Palermo four days later, making that port on 7 December. He then returned to New York on 11 February 1864.

Zephyr departed New York for Cadiz on 1 March 1864 and arrived on 25 March. Small sent a letter back to America describing the harrowing voyage. He recounted "very heavy weather for sixteen days" but that on 17 March a "violent hurricane" hit the ship, "with fearful violence through the afternoon, sea mountainous and very irregular, decks flooded with water most of the time." At 16:00 on that day, Small considered the situation serious enough to throw 124 barrels of petroleum overboard, which made for easier seakeeping. He went on to write "as night came on the gale seemed to increase, barque scudding under close reefed main topsail, seas breaking over her continually."

Around midnight, *Zephyr* shipped a heavy sea that staved in the skylight on the quarterdeck and flooded an aft cabin. Shortly afterwards, the vessel "shipped another sea over the main deck, staving boat, washing away side ports, breaking adrift spars, and water casks (all of which were lashed solid when the gale came on), also washing bulwarks partly away, tearing the battenings and tarpaulins from the main hatch."

Despite the storm damage, Small only stayed in Cadiz for a few days before sailing for Palermo, where he arrived on 3 April before sailing to New York on 21 May, eventually returning on 10 July.

Small then handed *Zephyr* over to one Captain Knowles, who left New York at some point in July for Malaga, arriving on 10 September. He remained there until 19 September, when he sailed for Cadiz and arrived after a quick transit, but left almost immediately for New York. Knowles had an eventful voyage back weathering "constant westerly gales" and he "lost topgallant mast, sprung topsail yard, stove boat, split sails, &c." Knowles made New York late in 1864, and Small resumed his tenure as master.

Zephyr's first trip of 1865 was to Cadiz, on 4 January. Small arrived on 28 January, after an unusually speedy crossing. On 8 February, he sailed for Messina, arriving on 20 February. Small sailed for Boston on 4 March, making Gibraltar on 26 March and putting in at his final destination on 24 April. The next few weeks must have been nostalgic for Small, who sold *Zephyr* to an unnamed party

at some point in August. A mysterious Captain Sparrow then took *Zephyr* from Boston to Malaga at the end of that month, arriving on 22 September. After several erroneous reports in London's *Shipping Gazette* concerning Sparrow's destination, it seems that he sailed from Malaga on 24 October. He was then "towed out" of the Straits of Gibraltar at the end of November, and took *Zephyr* on its fourth trip around the horn, eventually arriving in San Francisco on 19 March 1866 laden with whole, half, and quarter boxes of raisins.

Zephyr's adventures continued on 9 April 1866, when Sparrow turned over with a Captain J. M. Miller, who sailed for Port Otago, New Zealand. However, he had to return to San Francisco four days later, after having the misfortune to both spring a leak and have seaman Thomas Sheobard fall from the maintop gallant yard and break a leg. Miller eventually sailed on 29 April, laden with flour, wheat, timber, and fence pickets, arriving on 6 July.

Miller ingratiated himself in Port Otago by attending *The Daughter of the Regiment* play, and for vague reasons felt compelled to give a lecture titled "A Half Hour on the American War." *The Otago Daily Times* reported that "it was necessarily not what is generally understood by the term lecture, but it was a talk calculated to be instructive to the majority of Britons, and which was certainly entertaining, from its peculiar humour and style of delivery." Miller even treated the audience to popular songs associated with the American Civil War.

On 24 July, Miller left Port Otago in ballast for Newcastle, Australia, and arrived laden with coal at Lyttelton, south of Christchurch, on 9 September. Miller left Lyttelton for Newcastle, again in ballast, and was expected to make a round trip with coal, but instead turned up in Hong Kong on 15 December. Shipping intelligence reported that Miller remained in Hong Kong until some point after 15 March 1867, when he turned over with the *Zephyr*'s new master, Captain Snow.

Snow's departure date from Hong Kong remains unknown, but his first trip was to Saigon, Vietnam, returning to Hong Kong on 27 April 1876. Snow then sailed into Chefoo (present-day Yantai), China, at some point after 28 September, and finally arrived in San

Francisco on 8 February 1868 – *Zephyr* hadn't been in an American port since April 1866.

Snow left San Francisco on 19 March for *Zephyr*'s first trip to Victoria, British Columbia, putting in on 16 April. He then sailed for Boundary Bay, where he accidentally grounded *Zephyr* and then returned to Victoria to auction his cargo of lumber on 22 April. Local papers reported the vessel safely afloat again shortly thereafter.

Snow returned to San Francisco on 4 May. His mishap in Boundary Bay evidently didn't put him off *Zephyr*, as he purchased the ship shortly after arriving. However, he then handed captaincy to the San Francisco-based Captain Freeman Trask, who sailed for Umpqua, Oregon, on 28 May. He later reported at Port Ludlow, Washington, on 16 June – probably to load timber – and he sailed south to San Francisco on 24 June, arriving on 5 July. Trask then made another round trip between San Francisco and the Columbia River, arriving back in San Francisco on 24 August. Next, Trask voyaged north yet again, this time calling at Portland on 17 October, but was reported to be aground on Swan Island Bar on 24 October. Trask evidently refloated *Zephyr*, as he returned to San Francisco on 21 November. He sailed for Portland again on 11 December, but his return date is unknown.

Trask's first voyage of 1869 was to Steilacoom, Washington, and he returned to San Francisco on 1 April. He made the same trip in May, and then sailed for Victoria and Port Townsend, Washington, and returned before June. At the beginning of June, the barque *Oregon*, while under tow of the tug *Sol Thomas*, collided with *Zephyr*, while Trask was alongside San Francisco's Howard Street Wharf. Papers reported, "the stern of the *Oregon* struck the main rail of the *Zephyr* on the port side, carrying away a portion of it and breaking four stanchions." Between June and October, Trask conducted business around the Southern Gulf Islands and Puget Sound, calling at Steilacoom twice and also Victoria. He finally returned to San Francisco laden with lumber on 16 November. He sailed north for Port Townsend on 24 November, and returned to San Francisco on 27 January 1870.

Zephyr's first outbound voyage of 1870 began after Trask sailed north from San Buenaventura for Steilacoom on 3 May and arrived twenty-four days later. Trask then sailed for San Francisco on 10 June, arriving on 1 July laden with lumber. Trask next sailed on 22 July for Portland, arriving on 14 August. He returned to San Francisco near the end of September laden with produce, and sailed for Astoria on 3 October. He arrived twenty days later, and returned to San Francisco after a speedy eleven-day transit on 25 November.

Trask and his brother Alden must have spent the next month getting their affairs in order, as the *Zephyr* changed hands on the curious date of 24 December 1870, when Alden purchased the ship and registered it in San Francisco with his brother Freeman as Master. Curiously, he declared the total tonnage as 337, a marked difference from the initial 414 tons specified by the Assistant Deputy Surveyor in 1855. Was he trying to evade registration taxes by claiming his ship was actually another registered 337-ton former whaling barque also named *Zephyr*? Did he choose to complete his registration paperwork on Christmas Eve, when the port offices would have been minimally staffed, hoping that no one would realize that he was paying registration taxes on a vessel almost 75 tons larger than declared? In any case, the Trask brothers didn't dither: Freeman quietly slipped away from San Francisco on Christmas of 1870, bound for faraway Acajutla, El Salvador. Unfortunately for the Trask brothers, the scheme didn't pan out, and both men and *Zephyr* ended up in the following years Special Personal Property Delinquent Tax List.

Trask arrived in Acajutla on 28 January 1871, and returned to San Francisco at some point in the spring. He then sailed for Victoria on 12 June, arriving on 4 July. Loaded with 150 tons of merchandise, Trask had a frustrating northbound transit with "light adverse winds" to Cape Flattery, followed by a week stuck in irons at that same Cape. He sailed from that city to Newcastle Island "and commenced to load stone at the Newcastle quarries" on 12 July. Trask loaded his cargo for the rest of the month, eventually slipping on 1 August and making a swift transit to San Francisco, arriving on 14 August laden with 400 tons of granite and 14 tons of "old iron" for the renowned contractor Joseph Stickney Emery.

The New Hampshire-born Emery travelled to California

to strike his fortune in 1850, but became "the foremost builder of his time," with a portfolio of projects including San Francisco's Parrot Building, a quarry on present-day Yerba Buena Island, a dry dock at Mare Island Naval Shipyard, and the contract to provide the stone to build the San Francisco Mint. Emery had established an arrangement in 1869 with the Vancouver Coal Mining and Land Company to supply needed materials for the mint, which evolved into the successful Newcastle Island quarry.

During the latter half of August, Trask turned over with Captain Hipson, who left San Francisco on 29 August for Newcastle Island and arrived one month later. Hipson's first voyage did not go smoothly. On 8 October, Nanaimo authorities arrested a crewman for quarrelling with other members of the crew with a knife. At the same time, a legal dispute arose between Captain Hipson and a Nanaimo resident named Sacke over the price of timber allegedly used by Hipson. A constable went to *Zephyr* to serve a summons to Hipson, who refused to accept it. Instead of actually reading the summons to Hipson, the constable "threw it on the deck of the ship without having first read it to him," which Hipson interpreted as not having been served at all. He sailed shortly thereafter, leaving the summons unresolved and a crewman in jail.

Hipson returned to San Francisco in fall 1871, and again set sail for Newcastle Island from San Pedro on 11 November.

Loss

Hipson sailed from San Pedro on 11 November 1871, and Victoria's *Daily Colonist* reported on 29 December that *Zephyr* was two weeks overdue at the quarry. Hipson finally arrived on 30 January 1872. On 3 February, *Zephyr* was "loading stone at the quarry" along with the vessel *Orient*. A week later the same paper reported that "the *Zephyr* had finished loading stone and had got the columns safely in." Hipson departed the quarry on 12 February "loaded with a cargo of building stone for San Francisco." According to First Mate George Lusk, "the vessel was light, staunch and strong, well mannered, victualled and found in very respect fit to perform her said intended voyage." At 20:00 the same night, the wind veered from the southeast to the northeast, and at 01:00

on 13 February, "a heavy snowstorm set in during which time the best lookout was constantly kept on board." However, "owing to this snowstorm it was impossible to distinguish the land." According to Lusk, the crew

> tried to tack ship but she missed stays. Being afraid the vessel might be upon a lee shore, and upon descrying the land we tried to wear ship. There not being enough room to do so, we backed the halyards and tried to back her off. But not succeeding we let go the bower anchor which failed to hold and the vessel with a heavy sea running at the time on shore, struck on Mayne Island on a rocky part and commenced pounding heavily.

It was apparent to the crew that due to "the position in which the vessel lay she was injured in the starboard bilge."

Lusk further elaborated that

> immediately after the vessel struck the pumps were sounded and duly attended for a short time, but finding the water gaining rapidly we thought it useless to continue pumping and, in about half an hour after the vessel struck, on sounding we found four feet of water in the hold.

At this point the men realized that the tide was flooding, and the consensus appears to have been that the "vessel would sink" at high tide. Thus Hipson "gave orders for the crew to get their baggage and prepare to leave the ship at daylight, not thinking it safe to leave before." The crew clewed the sails and prepared a boat to take them off the wreck.

Then, "at about half past six the ship suddenly heeled over and turned from the starboard side to the port side offshore. All the crew thereupon made a rush for the boat and six succeeded in reaching her," including the chief mate, George Lusk, the second mate, John Johnson, and seamen Moses Mandevillle, John Alyward, Andrew Robertson, and Robert Wilson. Lusk reported that the men "remained by the wreck until daylight to ascertain what had become of the captain, the cook Francis Santons, and two seamen James Stewart and Phillip Gough." They found the cook clinging to a floating foreyard and rescued him, then went ashore and "travelled on the land as near as we could get to the wreck," finding Gough washed ashore "alive yet in a very exhausted state."

The men "remained on the coast near the wreck" until around 13:00 on 13 February, "when in order to obtain assistance, being destitute of food and the storm in some degree abating "they hiked to Plumpers Pass (present-day Active Pass) and "remained for that night in the house of a fisherman." The next day, Lusk, Mandeville, and Aylward returned to the wreck to determine the fate of Hipson and Stewart, "but notwithstanding every effort were unable to do so. We discovered the wreck lying as we believed in four fathoms of water, the topgallant, the royal masts being only above water."

For the next three days, the men hunkered down in the fisherman's house, "the weather being exceedingly boisterous," but set sail for Victoria in the fisherman's boat on 16 February. Johnson and Gough remained behind "to use their best effort to save if possible and portion of the wreck." Lusk further reported that "we six members of the crew, after great hardships and privation together with the fisherman who brought us down in his boat eventually reached Victoria on the evening of Sunday the 18th" and immediately set out for the American consul, who supplied the men with "clothing and necessitates" as they were "in a most destitute state and condition." The following day Lusk went to David Eckstein, the United States Consul at Victoria's Port, to formally describe the accident. The day after that, Lusk, Mandeville, and Aylward went to the Bastion Street office of attorney-at-law and notary public Robert Bishop to provide a statement under oath concerning the *Zephyr*'s loss.

Salvage

Victoria's *Daily Colonist* tied off the chronicle of the *Zephyr* on 21 February 1872 by reporting "the wrecked bark [sic] *Zephyr* will be abandoned. Her condition is hopeless. The survivors will sail in the *Prince Alfred* for San Francisco today." Although Victoria's O. T. Mullard purchased the wreck for $42.50 later that month, he never salvaged it. *Zephyr* lay undiscovered, 40 feet below the surface of a bustling waterway, for the next 104 years.

Search and Discovery

In 1976, Mayne Island's Gary LeTour and the UASBC began independent searches for the *Zephyr*.

The UASBC invited side-scan sonar expert Dr. Harold Edgerton of the Massachusetts Institute of Technology to participate in the search, under the University of British Columbia's Cecil H. and Ida Green Visiting Professor program. The UASBC chartered the 65-foot converted tug *Santa Rita* over 9-10 October 1976 to conduct searches for *Zephyr*. Multiple side-scan passes were made along the eastern side of Mayne Island between David's Cove and Edith Point. Divers went into the water twice to investigate potential targets. However, after two days of searching, nothing was found.

Zephyr side-scan search, 9 October, 1976, courtesy of UASBC Collection.

Gary LeTour located the undisturbed remains of the *Zephyr* in 12 m of water about halfway between Edith Point and David's Cove either on November 27 or December 27, 1976.

Armed with a wreck location map provided by Gary, the UASBC conducted its first dive on the site on 23 January 1977. This dive was an exploratory dive to locate the wreck and determine the extent of the site. On subsequent trips (27 March, 23-24 April, and 1-3 May, 1977), the UASBC surveyed the wreck and excavated some of the stern area. The survey results were plotted to produce a scaled site plan of the wreck.

A number of artifacts, such as *Zephyr*'s chronometer, sextant, navigation slates, ceramic ware, glassware, and various ship fittings were raised. Some of these artifacts are in the UASBC Collection and others are on display at the Mayne Island Museum. Unfortunately, the positions of the recovered artifacts were not plotted on the survey. During the survey work, there was some discussion about recovering the rudder, but in the end, it was left on site. The rudder was eventually raised and ended up at the Vancouver Maritime Museum, but it has since disappeared.

As more sport divers discovered the location of the wreck, the UASBC became concerned for the archaeological integrity of the site, and urged the provincial government to designate the *Zephyr* a Protected Heritage Site. The *Zephyr* was designated a Heritage Site on 3 February 1977 under the *Archaeological and Historic Sites Protection Act*.

In 1984 UASBC President David Griffiths proposed on behalf of the UASBC to raise some of the cargo of the *Zephyr* for display. At the time, the project was put on

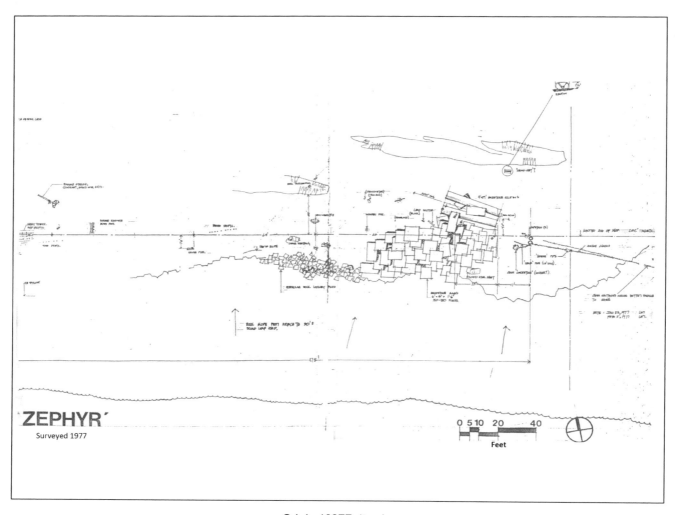

Original 1977 site plan.

hold due to lack of funds. In 1987 the plan was revived, and UASBC member Gary Bridges became the project director. This time, the UASBC received financial assistance from the Ministry of Environment and Parks and the Nanaimo Harbour Commission, which each contributed $8,500 towards the $17,000 cost of the project.

On the morning of 14 October 1987, a tugboat manoeuvred the 120-foot barge *McKenzie* of Fraser River Pile and Dredge with its 200-ton crane into position over the wreck site.

UASBC members had secured buoys on site in advance and jetted trenches under each column for the four heavy-duty lifting straps. At the end of the day, five blocks weighing 4-10 tons each had been raised, as well as the two 30-foot columns the *Zephyr* had carried. On 15 October, the barge and crane deposited one of the columns on Newcastle Island close to where it had been quarried. Four of the sandstone blocks were unloaded at Maffeo-Sutton Park in Nanaimo, which is the departure location for the ferry to Newcastle Island.

One of the smaller blocks was taken for display at the Mayne Island Museum by Gary LeTour, one of the original discoverers of the wreck.

The following week on 19 October, the remaining column from the *Zephyr*, thoroughly cleaned from a sand-blasting job, was installed at the Vancouver Maritime Museum with the help of a 120-ton crane.

Status

The UASBC tried diving the *Zephyr* as part of the Southern Gulf Islands re-inventory project on 20 September 2015. Unfortunately, the sea conditions were too rough to dive the site. This is not an unusual occurrence. The original Gulf Islands report remarks that "the sea conditions in the area of the wreck often consist of strong current flows which can make diving tricky." A further confounding issue when diving *Zephyr* is that the Fraser River sediment plume reaches the wreck in the spring, which can reduce the underwater visibility to less than 1 m.

The notes for this section are therefore dependent on observations made while diving the site on 23 August 2008. As discussed earlier, the wreck lies about halfway between Edith Point and David's Cove on the east side of Mayne Island at 48° 51.662' N by 123° 15.381' W

The remains of the *Zephyr* lie parallel to shore on mixed sand-shell and rock bottom. The wreckage is nestled between the sloping shore to the west and exposed underwater rock outcrops to the east. The hull is completely gone, the result of marine borers and tidal action over 147 years. Laminaria leaf kelp covers much of the bottom near the wreck, hiding many of the smaller artifacts. The wreckage lies on a 304° bearing bow to stern.

The overall site measures 84 m long by 20 m wide. A hawse pipe and anchor chain, mark the bow in 40 feet (12 m) of water. Astern of the hawse pipe is the capstan. Five m northwest of the capstan, the sandstone block cargo begins. The sandstone blocks extend towards the stern for 22 m and the width of the pile varies from 12 to 15 m. The blocks within the pile vary in size. The site plan records one sample which is 2.4 high by 1.8 wide by .45 m lone, while two of the recovered blocks at Maffeo-Sutton Park measure 2.1 m high by 1.15 m wide by 0.65 m long, m and 2.2 m high by 1.21 m wide and 0.62 m long.

Four sandstone blocks from *Zephyr* on display at Maffeo-Sutton Park. Photo courtesy of Bronwen Young.

Astern of the sandstone blocks, the bottom becomes increasingly sandy. Heavy timbers and drift bolts are found 54 m north of the sandstone blocks. These features mark the northernmost extremity of the wreck site. The rudder was located in this area before being recovered.

Some extant wood, brass drift bolts, and copper sheathing poke through the sand here and there in the intervening distance. Also in the stern area but to the north, is an object that looks like it may be part of the vessel's steering apparatus. Many smaller artifacts like lignum vitae rigging sheaths and deadeyes can be found in and around the sandstone cargo.

One final observation: the *Zephyr* was 38 m (125 feet) in length. The fact that the site measures 84 m (275 feet) in length suggests that as the wreck deteriorated the stern became separated from the main hull.

Conclusions/Recommendations

Despite the obvious diving activity and artifact removal at the site, the *Zephyr* has by no means completely lost its archaeological integrity. The 1982 report suggested that all artifacts raised before the site's designation as a Heritage Site, such as those on display at the Mayne Museum and Vancouver Maritime Museum, be properly inventoried and photographed. This was not done and should be a future priority.

The UASBC placed an educational plaque on the *Zephyr* in 1983, but its current whereabouts and condition are unknown. A follow-up dive should be carried out to determine the plaque's status. Finally, there is no interpretive information on the column at the Vancouver Maritime Museum. The UASBC recommends that we work with the museum to prioritize adding this information.

References

Beasley Tom. "*Zephyr*: A Grand Lift for the UASBC." *Foghorn,* (November 1987).

Beasley Tom. "View From the Chair." *Foghorn* (October 1987).

Boston Daily Advertiser, 11 September 1855.

Ibid., 11 February 1856.

Ibid., 15 January 1857.

Ibid., 25 April 1857.

Ibid., 4 May 1857.

Ibid., 26 February 1859.

Ibid., 29 July 1859.

Ibid., 12 August 1859.

Ibid., 24 October 1859.

Ibid., 8 December 1859.

Ibid., 9 January 1860.

Ibid., 20 January 1860.

Ibid., 25 January 1860.

Ibid., 8 March 1860.

Ibid., 5 April 1860.

Ibid., 4 January 1861.

Ibid., 5 March 1861.

Ibid., 8 June 1861.

Ibid., 19 September 1861.

Ibid., 17 October 1861.

Ibid., 17 February 1862.

Ibid., 26 February 1862.

Ibid., 8 March 1862.

Ibid., 12 June 1861.

Ibid., 14 August 1862.

Ibid., 9 October 1862.

Ibid., 20 October 1862.

Ibid., 1 December 1862

Ibid., 2 March 1863.

Ibid., 10 March 1863.

Ibid., 11 April 1863.

Ibid., 12 May 1863.

Ibid., 4 August 1863.

Ibid., 19 August 1863.

Ibid., 8 October 1863.

Ibid., 5 December 1863.

Ibid., 21 December 1863.

Ibid., 1 January 1864.

Ibid., 12 February 1864.

Ibid., 3 March 1864.

Ibid., 20 April 1864.

Ibid., 23 April 1864.

Ibid., 30 May 1864.

Ibid., 11 June 1864.

Ibid.,11 July 1864.

Ibid., 6 October 1864.

Ibid., 12 October 1864.

Ibid., 19 October 1864.

Ibid., 11 November 1864.

Ibid., 5 January 1865.

Ibid., 20 February 1865.

Ibid., 6 March 1865.

Ibid., 20 March 1865.

Ibid., 3 April 1865.

Ibid., 18 April 1865.

Ibid., 25 April 1865.

Ibid., 10 August 1865.

Ibid., 25 August 1865.

Ibid., 13 October 1865.

Ibid., 1 December 1865.

Ibid., 16 February 1867.

Ibid., 15 May 1876.

Ibid., 13 September 1867.

Ibid., 14 April 1868.

Ibid., 16 May 1868.

Ibid., 27 May 1868.

Ibid., 28 May 1868.

Ibid., 25 July 1868.

Ibid., 10 September 1868.

Ibid., 6 November 1868.

Ibid., 11 November 1868.

Ibid., 9 December 1868.

Ibid., 31 December 1868.

Ibid., 14 October 1869.

Ibid., 4 December 1869.

Ibid., 1 August 1870.

Ibid., 2 August 1870.

Boston Daily Atlas, 1 April 1856.

Ibid., 12 April 1856.

Ibid., 16 May 1856.

Ibid., 31 May 1856.

British Columbia Designated Heritage Sites Registry, Province of British Columbia, Ministry of Tourism, Archaeology Branch, 1993.

Bruce Herald, 12 July 1866.

Charleston Courier, Tri-Weekly, 16 April 1859.

The Charleston Mercury, 15 January 1858.

Daily Alta California, 1 June 1869.

Ibid., 8 May 1870.

Ibid., 4 October 1870.

Ibid., 26 November 1870.

Ibid., 25 December 1870.

Ibid., 2 September 1871.

Ibid., 13 June 1871.

Ibid., 7 July 1871.

Ibid., 11 November 1871.

Daily British Colonist, 22 April 1868.

Ibid., 24 June 1869.

Ibid., 5 July 1871.

Ibid., 19 July 1871.

Ibid., 10 August 1871.

Ibid., 14 August 1871.

Ibid., 30 September.

Ibid., 12 October 1871.

Ibid., 10 February 1872.

Ibid., 7 January 1973.

Daily Evening Bulletin, 19 April 1866.

Ibid., 8 February 1868.

Ibid., 16 April 1868.

Ibid., 20 April 1868.

Ibid., 27 June 1868.

Ibid., 7 April 1869.

Ibid., 16 November 1869.

Ibid., 28 May 1870.

Ibid., 16 August 1870.

Ibid., 20 September 1870.

Ibid., 30 August 1871.

Deyo, Simeon, ed. *History of Barnstable County*. (New York: H. W. Blake & Co., 1890), 627.

Zephyr Vertical Ship's File, Enrollment Document from the Port of Boston and Charlestown, 18 August 1855, Vancouver Maritime Museum

Griffiths, David W. "Zephyr" *Foghorn*, (March 1985),3

Ibid., Jan 1985.

Ibid., Oct 1984.

Ibid., July 1978.

Ibid., Aug 1977.

Ibid., Feb 1977.

Knoblock, Glenn A. *The American Clipper Ship, 1845-1920: A Comprehensive History with a Listing of Builders and Their Ships*. (Jefferson: McFarland & Company, 2014), 293.

McDaniel, Neil. "Raising the Past." *Diver Magazine*, (February 1988), 18-19.

McMartin, Pete. "Diver Locates 100-Year Old Wreck." *The Vancouver Sun*, 25 January 1977.

Morrison, Samuel Elliot. *The Maritime History of Massachusetts: 1783-1860*. (Boston: Northeastern University Press, 1979), 191.

North America and United States Gazette, 10 February 1863.

Ibid., 13 August 1863.

Ibid., 13 November 1865.

Ibid., 28 June 1867.

Official Deposition of Chief Mate George Lusk to Robert Bishop, 20 February 1872.

Padmore, Tim. "Electronic Wizard Hunts for Shipwreck Treasure." *The Vancouver Sun*, 13 October, 1976.

Press, Volume X, Issue 1099, 10 September 1866.

Ibid., Issue 1215, 20 September 1866.

San Francisco Call, 23 January 1909.

The New York Herald, 17 February 1857.

Ibid., 7 June 1857.

Ibid., 25 July 1857.

Ibid., 25 August 1857.

Ibid., 25 October 1857.

Ibid., 22 November 1857.

Ibid., 2 December 1857.

Ibid., 14 June 1858.

Ibid., 12 August 1859.

Ibid., 30 August 1859.

Ibid., 23 December 1859.

Ibid., 9 February 1860.

Ibid., 27 February 1860.

Ibid., 9 March 1860.

Ibid., 15 September 1860.

Ibid., 26 September 1860.

Ibid., 4 January 1861.

Ibid., 12 February 1861.

Ibid., 23 October 1861.

Ibid., 8 November 1861.

Ibid., 3 July 1863.

The Otago Daily Times, 21 July 1866.

Ibid., 25 July 1866.

Zephyr Vertical Ship's File, Registration Document for the Port of San Francisco, 24 December 1870, Vancouver Maritime Museum.